POETRY OF THE
FIRST WORLD WAR

William Orpen, 'The Thinker on the Butte de Warlencourt'

POETRY OF
THE FIRST
WORLD WAR

COLLECTOR'S POETRY LIBRARY

This edition first published in 2004 by
COLLECTOR'S POETRY LIBRARY
an imprint of CRW Publishing Limited
69 Gloucester Crescent, London NW1 7EG

ISBN 1 904919 39 1

This edition copyright © CRW Publishing Limited 2004

Peter Harness has asserted his right under the Copyright
Designs and Patents Act 1988 to be identified as the author of
the Introduction.

2 4 6 8 10 9 7 5 3 1

Typeset in Perpetua by Bookcraft Ltd,
Stroud, Gloucestershire, UK

Printed and bound in China by Imago

Contents

William Orpen, '"Good-bye-ee": Cassel'

Introduction

And all this madness, all this rage, all this flaming death of our civilisation and our hopes, has been brought about because a set of official gentlemen, living luxurious lives, mostly stupid, and all without imagination or heart, have chosen that it should occur rather than that any one of them should suffer some infinitesimal rebuff to his country's pride.

Bertrand Russell (1914)

IN his impassioned attack on the declaration of war in August 1914, the philosopher Bertrand Russell was something of a lone voice. At the time, Great Britain was riding a wave of martial and Imperial enthusiasm, and the people very much wanted a conflict. Germany, heavily remilitarised during the reign of Kaiser Wilhelm II, had begun massing its army on the border with Belgium, and it seemed clear that an invasion was imminent. In response to this, the British Prime Minister, Herbert Asquith, had instructed his Foreign Secretary, Edward Grey, to issue an ultimatum: if Germany did not give Belgium an assurance of safety, then Britain would intervene on her side, and war would be declared. The deadline for this assurance was 11pm on 4 August 1914: a warm Bank Holiday weekend, in a long and pleasant summer, in the dog-days of the British Empire.

No such assurance was given, and crowds gathered in Trafalgar Square and outside Buckingham Palace to cheer the announcement of war. Most people believed that it would 'all be over by Christmas': that they were going to teach the Germans a swift lesson, and then get back to the business of running the great British empire. They were wrong.

In these early stages, poetry played a considerable part in drumming up support for the conflict. The first war poem to be printed (in *The Times* on 6 August 1914), was William Watson's 'To the Troubler of the World', a sneering piece of invective by a minor writer, reprinted here for its curiosity value more than its poetic worth. Watson was soon joined by laureates such as Robert Bridges and Rudyard Kipling, enjoining the men of England to 'stand up and meet the war' because 'the Hun is at the gate'. War poetry quickly began to thrive. Sir Henry Newbolt, who had long been a writer of martial, nationalistic verse, assembled a hasty collection from his back catalogue (from which 'Clifton Chapel' is taken), which sold 70,000 copies within a few weeks. Keen to exploit this popular thirst for rousing verse, the Liberal government set up the 'Secret War Propaganda Bureau': an organisation whose brief was, in part, to organise artists and writers to publicly support the cause. From this group came many of the poems collected here: those who attended its meetings included Thomas Hardy, John Galsworthy, Robert Bridges, Rudyard Kipling and Laurence Binyon (he who wrote 'At the going down of the sun and in the morning / We will remember them').

However, in these early stages of the conflict, younger writers were beginning to emerge as well: men of fighting age who were writing of life on the front line, and whom we now think of as the First World War Poets. Perhaps the most famous poem of the entire conflict, Rupert Brooke's 'The Soldier' ('If I should die, think only this of me...') was written in the early days of the war, when Brooke was unknown to the public. Although he was ambivalent about the conflict to begin with, he soon joined up (in fact, on the recommendation of Winston Churchill), and threw himself wholly into thoughts of military glory: afflicted, like so many of his class, generation and schooling, with an inflated admiration of heroic sacrifice. He died early in 1915, having seen almost no conflict, of blood-poisoning, on his ship in the Greek islands. Yet he was painted as a hero: his poems celebrated the notion of giving one's life for one's country, and were seized on by the propagandists. His work became hugely popular: after his death his poems were reprinted, on average, every eight weeks throughout the war.

Brooke is perhaps the only major War Poet who did not experience the horror that the conflict became, and so never moved away from Newbolt-style celebration of glorious warfare. Most of the other writers in this volume – even those, like Hardy and Kipling, who did not see active service – found their attitudes dramatically altered as the war got under way, and the futility and senselessness of the slaughter became all too apparent.

Of the poets who emerged during the conflict, the most highly regarded are Wilfred Owen and Siegfried Sassoon, followed closely by Isaac Rosenberg and Edward Thomas. These were original and individual poetic voices, with much to contribute to the literary and social development of Great Britain. Owen's verse may be characterised by a sentimental, almost Romantic, tenderness, which renders the horrors of war even more bitter by contrast. Sassoon is altogether more spiky and distressing. His poems are shot through with anger and frustration, yet they also have a strong religious and spiritual yearning, and were highly controversial at the time. Rosenberg's work is experimental, forceful and direct: he and Sassoon are perhaps the most distinct and exciting new voices to emerge during the war. Thomas's poems are suffused with depression and melancholia; yet they are lyrical, and evoke a pastoral yearning for his home in England.

Of these four great writers, only Sassoon lived to see the Armistice. It may seem narrow-minded to mourn their loss more than any of the other nine million who died in the Great War. However, as living memory of the conflict fades away, the words of these brilliant, talented young men, and their untimely deaths, seem increasingly to encapsulate the wastefulness of it all. They seem to represent a whole generation of potential writers, poets, dramatists, novelists, actors, politicians, scientists, inventors, healers, husbands, lovers, fathers and grandfathers: a generation which clearly had so much to give and to achieve, and which was, as Kipling said, 'defrauded' of the chance.

Also included here are several poems from women writers: May Wedderburn Cannan, Teresa Hooley, Winifred Letts and Charlotte Mew. The War Poets have long been thought of as an exclusively male group. Thankfully, we are now able to access new poetic perspectives on the conflict: those of the grieving and anxious mother, the bereaved wife or fiancée, the front-line nurse, or simply the concerned woman on the home front. These give a refreshing new perspective on the war, and help to put the work of the male poets into different contexts and sharper relief.

Peter Harness

Albin Egger-Linz, 'Den Namenlosen, 1914' ('Those
Who Have Lost Their Names, 1914') (1916)

Anthem for Dead Youth.

What passing-bells for you who die in herds?
  — Only the monstrous anger of the guns!
  — Only the stuttering rifles' rattled words
Can patter out your hasty orisons.
No chants for you, nor balms, nor wreaths, nor bells,   chorus
  Nor any voice of mourning, save the choirs.   shells
  And long-drawn bugle choirs of wailing shells;
  The shrill demented choirs of wailing shells;
  And bugles calling for you from sad shires.

What candles may we hold to speed you all?
  Not in the hands of boys, but in their eyes
  Shall shine the holy lights of long goodbyes.
The pallor of girls' brows shall be your pall;   comrades'
  Your flowers, the tenderness of mortal minds,
  And each slow dusk, a drawing down of blinds.

                              Wilfred Owen.

Manuscript of Wilfred Owen's 'Anthem for Dommed Youth'

Poetry of the First World War

*Only the dead have
seen the end of war.*

George Santayana

Richard Aldington (1892–1962)

THE LOVER

THOUGH I have had friends
   And a beautiful love
There is one lover I await above all.
She will not come to me
In the time of soft plum-blossoms
When the air is gay with birds singing
And the sky is a delicate caress;
She will come
From the midst of a vast clamour
With a mist of stars about her
And great beckoning plumes of smoke
Upon her leaping horses.

And she will bend suddenly and clasp me;
She will clutch me with fierce arms
And stab me with a kiss like a wound
That bleeds slowly.

But though she will hurt me at first
In her strong gladness
She will soon soothe me gently
And cast upon me an unbreakable sleep
Softly for ever.

BOMBARDMENT

Four days the earth was rent and torn
   By bursting steel,
The houses fell about us;
Three nights we dared not sleep,
Sweating, and listening for the imminent crash
Which meant our death.

The fourth night every man,
Nerve-tortured, racked to exhaustion,
Slept, muttering and twitching,
While the shells crashed overhead.

The fifth day there came a hush;
We left our holes
And looked above the wreckage of the earth
To where the white clouds moved in silent lines
Across the untroubled blue.

Anonymous

WHEN THIS BLOODY WAR IS OVER

To the tune of 'What a Friend I Have in Jesus'

WHEN this bloody war is over,
Oh, how happy I shall be!
When I get my civvy clothes on
No more soldiering for me.
No more church parades on Sunday,
No more asking for a pass.
I shall tell the Sergeant-Major
To stick his passes up his arse.

When this bloody war is over,
Oh, how happy I shall be!
When I get my civvy clothes on
No more soldiering for me.
I shall sound my own revally,
I shall make my own tattoo.
No more N.C.O.s to curse me,
No more bleeding Army stew.

N.C.O.s will all be navvies,
Privates ride in motor cars.
N.C.O.s will smoke their Woodbines,
Privates puff their big cigars.
No more standing-to in trenches,
Only one more church parade.
No more shivering on the firestep,
No more Tickler's marmalade.

I DON'T WANT TO BE A SOLDIER

To the tune 'On Sunday I Walk Out With a Soldier'

I DON'T want to be a soldier,
I don't want to go to war.
I'd rather stay at home,
Around the streets to roam,
And live on the earnings of a well-paid whore.
I don't want a bayonet up my arse-hole,
I don't want my ballocks shot away.
I'd rather stay in England,
In merry merry England,
And fornicate my bloody life away.

Laurence Binyon (1869–1943)

FOR THE FALLEN

WITH proud thanksgiving, a mother for her children,
England mourns for her dead across the sea.
Flesh of her flesh they were, spirit of her spirit,
Fallen in the cause of the free.

Solemn the drums thrill; Death august and royal
Sings sorrow up into immortal spheres.
There is music in the midst of desolation
And a glory that shines upon our tears.

They went with songs to the battle; they were young,
Straight of limb, true of eye, steady and aglow.
They were staunch to the end against odds uncounted;
They fell with their faces to the foe.

They shall not grow old, as we that are left grow old:
Age shall not weary them, nor the years condemn.
At the going down of the sun and in the morning
We will remember them.

They mingle not with their laughing comrades again;
They sit no more at familiar tables of home;
They have no lot in our labour of the day-time;
They sleep beyond England's foam.

But where our desires are and our hopes profound,
Felt as a well-spring that is hidden from sight,
To the innermost heart of their own land they are known
As the stars are known to the Night;

As the stars that shall be bright when we are dust,
Moving in marches upon the heavenly plain;
As the stars that are starry in the time of our darkness,
To the end, to the end, they remain.

John Peele Bishop (1892–1944)

IN THE DORDOGNE

WE stood up before day
      and shaved by metal mirrors
in the faint flame of a faulty candle.

And we hurried down the wide stone stairs
with a clirr of spurr chains
on stone. And we thought
when the cocks crew
that the ghosts of a dead dawn
would rise and be off. But they stayed
under the window, crouched on the staircase,
the window now the colour of morning.

The colonel slept in the bed of Sully,
slept on: but we descended
and saw in a niche in the white wall
a Virgin and child, serene
who were stone: we saw sycamore:
three aged mages
scattering gifts of gold.
But when the wind blew, there were autumn odours
and the shadowed trees
had the dapplings of young fawns.

And each day one died or another
died: each week we sent out thousands
that returned by hundreds
wounded or gassed. And those that died
we buried close to the old wall
within a stone's throw of Perigord
under the tower of the troubadours.

And because we had courage;
because there was courage and youth
ready to be wasted; because we endured
and were prepared for all the endurance;
we thought something must come of it:
that the Virgin would raise her child and smile;
the trees gather up their gold and go;
that courage would avail something
and something we had never lost
be regained through wastage, by dying,
by burying the others under the English tower.

The colonel slept on in the bed of Sully
under the ravelling curtains: the leaves fell
and were blown away: the young men rotted
under the shadow of the tower
in a land of small clear silent streams
where the coming on of evening is
the letting down of blue and azure veils
over the clear and silent streams
delicately bordered by poplars.

Edmund Blunden (1896–1974)

REPORT ON EXPERIENCE

I HAVE been young, and now am not too old;
And I have seen the righteous forsaken,
His health, his honour and his quality taken.
This is not what we were formerly told.

I have seen a green country, useful to the race,
Knocked silly with guns and mines, its villages vanished,
Even the last rat and the last kestrel banished –
God bless us all, this was peculiar grace.

I knew Seraphina; Nature gave her hue,
Glance, sympathy, note, like one from Eden.
I saw her smile warp, heard her lyric deaden;
She turned to harlotry; – this I took to be new.

Say what you will, our God sees how they run.
These disillusions are His curious proving
That He loves humanity and will go on loving;
Over there are faith, life, virtue in the sun.

THE MIDNIGHT SKATERS

THE hop-poles stand in cones,
   The icy pond lurks under,
The pole-tops steeple to the thrones
Of stars, sound gulfs of wonder;
But not the tallest thee, 'tis said,
Could fathom to this pond's black bed.

Then is not death at watch
Within those secret waters?
What wants he but to catch
Earth's heedless sons and daughters?
With but a crystal parapet
Between, he has his engines set.

Then on, blood shouts, on, on,
Twirl, wheel and whip above him,
Dance on this ball-floor thin and wan,
Use him as though you love him;
Court him, elude him, reel and pass,
And let him hate you through the glass.

VLAMERTINGHE: PASSING THE CHATEAU

' AND all her silken flanks with garlands drest' –
But we are coming to the sacrifice.
Must those have flowers who are not yet gone West?
May those have flowers who live with death and lice?
This must be the flowerist place
That earth allows; the queenly face
Of the proud mansion borrows grace for grace
Spite of those brute guns lowing at the skies.

Bold great daisies' golden lights,
Bubbling roses' pinks and whites –
Such a gay carpet! poppies by the million;
Such damask! such vermilion!
But if you ask me, mate, the choice of colour
Is scarcely right; this red should have been duller.

Preparations for Victory

My soul, dread not the pestilence that hags
The valley; flinch not you, my body young,
At these great shouting smokes and snarling jags
Of fiery iron; as yet may not be flung
The dice that claims you. Manly move among
These ruins, and what you must do, do well;
Look, here are gardens, there mossed boughs are hung
With apples whose bright cheeks none might excel,
And there's a house as yet unshattered by a shell.

'I'll do my best,' the soul makes sad reply,
'And I will mark the yet unmurdered tree,
The tokens of dear homes that court the eye,
And yet I see them not as I would see.
Hovering between, a ghostly enemy.
Sickens the light, and poisoned, withered, wan,
The least defiled turns desperate to me.'
The body, poor unpitied Caliban,
Parches and sweats and grunts to win the name of Man.

Days or eternities like swelling waves
Surge on, and still we drudge in this dark maze;
The bombs and coils and cans by strings of slaves
Are borne to serve the coming day of days;
Pale sleep in slimy cellars scarce allays
With its brief blank the burden. Look, we lose;
The sky is gone, the lightless, drenching haze
Of rainstorms chills the bone; earth, air are foes,
The black fiend leaps brick-red as life's last picture goes.

Robert Bridges (1844–1930)

LORD KITCHENER

UNFLINCHING hero, watchful to foresee
     And face thy country's peril wheresoe'er,
Directing war and peace with equal care,
Till by long toil ennobled thou wert he
Whom England call'd and bade 'Set my arm free
To obey my will and save my honour fair,' –
What day the foe presumed on her despair
And she herself had trust in none but thee:

Among Herculean deeds the miracle
That mass'd the labour of ten years in one
Shall be thy monument. Thy work was done
Ere we could thank thee; and the high sea swell
Surgeth unheeding where thy proud ship fell
By the lone Orkneys, at the set of sun.

Rupert Brooke (1887–1930)

FRAGMENT

I STRAYED about the deck, an hour, to-night
Under a cloudy moonless sky; and peeped
In at the windows, watched my friends at table,
Or playing cards, or standing in the doorway,
Or coming out into the darkness. Still
No one could see me.

   I would have thought of them
– Heedless, within a week of battle – in pity,
Pride in their strength and in the weight and firmness
And link'd beauty of bodies, and pity that
This gay machine of splendour'ld soon be broken,
Thought little of, pashed, scattered ...

   Only, always,
I could see them – against the lamplight – pass
Like coloured shadows, thinner than filmy glass,
Slight bubbles, fainter than the wave's faint light,
That broke to phosphorus out in the night,
Perishing things and strange ghosts – soon to die
To other ghosts – this one, or that, or I.

1914 (I)

PEACE

Now, God be thanked
                    Who has matched us with his hour,
And caught our youth, and wakened us from sleeping,
With hand made sure, clear eye, and sharpened power,
To turn, as swimmers into cleanness leaping,
Glad from a world grown old and cold and weary,
Leave the sick hearts that honour could not move,
And half-men, and their dirty songs and dreary,
And all the little emptiness of love!

Oh! we, who have known shame,
                    we have found release there,
Where there's no ill, no grief, but sleep is mending,
Naught broken save the body, lost but breath;
Nothing to shake the laughing heart's long peace there
But only agony, and that has ending;
And the worst friend and enemy is but Death.

1914 (V)

THE SOLDIER

IF I should die, think only this of me:
That there's some corner of a foreign field
That is for ever England. There shall be
In that rich earth a richer dust concealed;
A dust whom England bore, shaped, made aware,
Gave, once, her flowers to love, her ways to roam,
A body of England's, breathing English air,
Washed by the rivers, blest by suns of home.

And think, this heart, all evil shed away,
A pulse in the eternal mind, no less
Gives somewhere back the thoughts by England given;
Her sights and sounds; dreams happy as her day;
And laughter, learnt of friends; and gentleness,
In hearts at peace, under an English heaven.

May Wedderburn Cannan (1893–1973)

LAMPLIGHT

WE planned to shake the world together, you and I.
   Being young, and very wise;
Now in the light of the green shaded lamp
Almost I see your eyes
Light with the old gay laughter; you and I
Dreamed greatly of an Empire in those days,
Setting our feet upon laborious ways,
And all you asked of fame
Was crossed swords in the Army List;
My Dear, against your name.

We planned a great Empire together, you and I,
Bound only by the sea;
Now in the quiet of a chill Winter's night
Your voice comes hushed to me
Full of forgotten memories: you and I
Dreamed great dreams of our future in those days,
Setting our feet on undiscovered ways,
And all I asked of fame
A scarlet cross on my breast, my Dear,
For the swords by your name.

We shall never shake the world together, you and I,
For you gave your life away;
And I think my heart was broken by war,
Since on a summer day
You took the road we never spoke of; you and I
Dreamed greatly of an Empire in those days;
You set your feet upon the Western ways
And have no need of fame –
There's a scarlet cross on my breast, my Dear,
And a torn cross with your name.

F.S. Flint (1885–1960)

LAMENT

THE young men of the world
Are condemned to death.
They have been called up to die
For the crime of their fathers.

The young men of the world,
The growing, the ripening fruit,
Have been torn from their branches,
While the memory of the blossom
Is sweet in women's hearts;
They have been cast for a cruel purpose
Into the mashing-press and furnace.

The young men of the world
Look into each other's eyes,
And read there the same words:
Not yet! Not yet!
But soon perhaps, and perhaps certain.

The young men of the world
No longer possess the road:
The road possesses them.
They no longer inherit the earth:
The earth inherits them.
They are no longer the masters of fire:
Fire is their master;
They serve him, he destroys them.
They no longer rule the waters:
The genius of the seas
Has invented a new monster,
And they fly from its teeth.
They no longer breathe freely:
The genius of the air
Has contrived a new terror
That rends them into pieces.

The young men of the world
Are encompassed with death
He is all about them
In a circle of fire and bayonets.

Weep, weep, o women,
And old men break your hearts.

Ford Madox Ford (1873–1939)

THAT EXPLOIT OF YOURS

I MEET two soldiers sometimes here in Hell
The one, with a tear in the seat of his red pantaloons
Was stuck by a pitchfork,
Climbing a wall to steal apples.

The second has a seeming silver helmet,
Having died from the fall of his horse on some tram-lines
In Dortmund.

These two
Meeting in the vaulted and vaporous caverns of Hell
Exclaim always in identical tones:
'I at least have done my duty
                     to Society and the Fatherland!'
It is strange how the cliché prevails ...
For I will bet my hat that you who sent me here to Hell
Are saying the selfsame words at this very moment
Concerning that exploit of yours.

John Galsworthy (1867–1933)

Valley of the Shadow

God, I am travelling out to death's sea,
I, who exulted in sunshine and laughter,
Dreamed not of dying – death is such waste of me! –
  Grant me one prayer: Doom not the hereafter
Of mankind to war, as though I had died not –
  I who, in battle, my comrade's arm linking,
Shouted and sang – life in my pulses hot
  Throbbing and dancing! Let not my sinking
In dark be for naught, my death a vain thing!
  God, let me know it the end of man's fever!
Make my last breath a bugle call, carrying
  Peace o'er the valleys and cold hills for ever!

Wilfrid Gibson (1878–1962)

Mad

Neck-deep in mud,
  He mowed and raved –
He who had braved
The field of blood –
And as a lad
Just out of school
Yelled – April Fool!
And laughed like mad.

BREAKFAST

WE ate our breakfast lying on our backs
    Because the shells were screeching overhead.
I bet a rasher to a loaf of bread
That Hull United would beat Halifax
When Jimmy Stainthorpe played full-back instead
Of Billy Bradford. Ginger raised his head
And cursed, and took the bet, and dropt back dead.
We ate our breakfast lying on our backs
Because the shells were stretching overhead.

MARK ANDERSON

ON the low table by the bed
    Where it was set aside last night,
Beyond the bandaged lifeless head,
It glitters in the morning light;

And as the hours of watching pass,
I cannot sleep, I cannot think,
But only gaze upon the glass
Of water that he could not drink.

Julian Grenfell (1888–1915)

INTO BATTLE

THE naked earth is warm with Spring,
     And with green grass and bursting trees
Leans to the sun's gaze glorying,
And quivers in the sunny breeze;
And life is Colour and Warmth and Light,
And a striving evermore for these;
And he is dead who will not fight;
And who dies fighting has increase.

The fighting man shall from the sun
Take warmth, and life from glowing earth;
Speed with the light-foot winds to run
And with the trees to newer birth;
And find, when fighting shall be done,
Great rest, and fullness after dearth.

All the bright company of Heaven
Hold him in their bright comradeship,
The Dog-Star, and the Sisters Seven,
Orion's belt and sworded hip.

The woodland trees that stand together,
They stand to him each one a friend;
They gently speak in the windy weather;
They guide to valley and ridge's end.

The kestrel hovering by day,
And the little owls that call by night,
Bid him be swift and keen as they,
As keen of ear, as swift of sight.

The blackbird sings to him: 'Brother, brother,
If this be the last song you shall sing,
Sing well, for you may not sing another;
Brother, sing.'

In dreary doubtful waiting hours,
Before the brazen frenzy starts,
The horses show him nobler powers;
O patient eyes, courageous hearts!

And when the burning moment breaks,
And all things else are out of mind,
And only joy of battle takes
Him by the throat and makes him blind,

Through joy and blindness he shall know,
Not caring much to know, that still
Nor lead nor steel shall reach him, so
That it be not the Destined Will.

The thundering line of battle stands,
And in the air Death moans and sings;
But Day shall clasp him with strong hands,
And Night shall fold him in soft wings.

Ivor Gurney (1890–1937)

TO HIS LOVE

He's gone, and all our plans
Are useless indeed.
We'll walk no more on Cotswold
Where the sheep feed
Quietly and take no heed.
His body that was so quick
Is not as you
Knew it, on Severn river
Under the blue
Driving our small boat through.
You would not know him now...
But still he died
Nobly, so cover him over
With violets of pride
Purple from Severn side.
Cover him, cover him soon!
And with thick-set
Masses of memoried flowers-
Hide that red wet
Thing I must somehow forget.

Félix Vallotton, 'Le Plateau de Bolante' ('Bolante Plateau') (1917)

THE BOHEMIANS

CERTAIN people would not clean their buttons,
　Nor polish buckles after latest fashions,
Preferred their hair long, putties comfortable,
Barely escaping hanging, indeed hardly able;
In Bridge and smoking without army cautions
Spending hours that sped like evil for quickness,
(While others burnished brasses, earned promotions)
These were those ones who jested in the trench,
While others argued of army ways, and wrenched
What little soul they had still further from shape,
And died off one by one, or became officers
Without the first of dream, the ghost of notions
Of ever becoming soldiers, or smart and neat,
Surprised as ever to find the army capable
Of sounding 'Lights out' to break a game of Bridge,
As to fear candles would set a barn alight.
In Artois or Picardy they lie – free of useless fashions.

SONG

ONLY the wanderer
　Knows England's graces,
Or can see anew clear
Familiar faces.

And who loves joy as he
That dwells in shadows?
Do not forget me quite,
O Severn meadows.

THE TARGET

I SHOT him, and it had to be
One of us! 'Twas him or me.
'Couldn't be helped' and none can blame
Me, for you would do the same.

My mother, she can't sleep for fear
Of what might be a-happening here
To me. Perhaps it might be best
To die, and set her fears at rest.

For worst is worst, and worry's done.
Perhaps he was the only son …
Yet God keeps still, and does not say
A word of guidance anyway.

Well, if they get me, first I'll find
That boy, and tell him all my mind,
And see who felt the bullet worst,
And ask his pardon, if I durst.

All's a tangle. Here's my job.
A man might rave, or shout, or sob;
And God He takes no sort of heed.
This is a bloody mess indeed.

THE SILENT ONE

WHO died on the wires, and hung there,
                                    one of two –
Who for his hours of life had chattered through
Infinite lovely chatter of Bucks accent:
Yet faced unbroken wires; stepped over, and went
A noble fool, faithful to his stripes – and ended.
But I weak, hungry, and willing only for the chance
Of line – to fight in the line, lay down under unbroken
Wires, and saw the flashes and kept unshaken,
Till the politest voice – a finicking accent, said:
'Do you think you might crawl through, there:
                                    there's a hole.'
Darkness, shot at: I smiled, as politely replied –
'I'm afraid not, Sir.' There was no hole
                                    no way to be seen
Nothing but chance of death, after tearing of clothes
Kept flat, and watched the darkness,
                                    hearing bullets whizzing –
And thought of music – and swore
                                    deep heart's deep oaths
(Polite to God) and retreated and came on again,
Again retreated – and a second time faced the screen.

STRANGE HELLS

THERE are strange Hells within the minds War made
Not so often, not so humiliating afraid
As one would have expected —
                              the racket and fear guns made.

One Hell the Gloucester soldiers they quite put out;
Their first bombardment, when in combined black shout
Of fury, guns aligned, they ducked low their heads
And sang with diaphragms fixed beyond all dreads,
That tin and stretched-wire tinkle, that blither of tune;
'*Après la guerre fini*' till Hell all had come down,
Twelve-inch, six-inch, and eighteen pounders
                              hammering Hell's thunders.

Where are they now on State-doles,
                              or showing shop patterns
Or walking town to town sore in borrowed tatterns
Or begged. Some civic routine one never learns.
The heart burns — but has to keep out of face
                              how heart burns.

TOBACCO

WHEN tobacco came, when Raleigh did first bring in
The unfabled herb, the plant of peace, the king
Of comfort-bringers, then indeed new hope
Came to the host of poets – with new scope,
New range of power, since henceforth one might sit
Midnight-on and still further, while the war of wit
More kindly became and coloured till dawn came in
Piercing shutter chinks with pale daylight thin.

Raleigh he knew, but could not the impossible
War of swift steel and hurtled bronze foretell,
Nor the imaginary hurt on the body's vessel;
Nor how tobacco then would steady disastered
Nerves, courage by grey terror almost mastered.
Gloucester men, half a day more, would hide
Five cigarettes, and matches well inside
Their breasts, the one thing unsodden, while despair
Dripped incessantly without interest from the air;
Or go supperless
The better next day's tobacco taste to bless.
Wonder at fogs, stars, posts till headaches came
Those chief of trouble-comforts still the same.
Watch Verey-lights, sandbags,
                              grasses, rifle-sights, mud –
Crampt in uncouth postures men crouched or stood –
A Woodbine breakfast inspiring the blood.

Or in those caves of dug-outs, men taking lazily
Smoke in luxuriously, of Woodbines easily.
For one stroke forgiving fate and its so mazily
Self-entangled knots. Easing the strained back,
Somehow or other slipping unseen from the rack
Into tobacco scent, or savour or look;
The divine virtue of some contenting book
Multiplying; or in the sunniest quiet resting
Loll into restlessness or sleepy jesting.
Tobacco truly taken, as a thing.

Tobacco tasted exactly; in waves or ring
Noted; tobacco blown to the wind, or watched
Melt into ether's farthest smoother unmatched.
Keen sentries whiffing surreptitiously,
Sly fatigue parties hidden from scrutiny,
Last breath favours begged desperately.

Over all the breath of the airy vapour is known,
Life's curtain rises on it and Death's trembles down.
Heroism has taken it for a sufficient crown.

When I think of the Ark slapping hopeless waters –
Of neas's sailors cursed with unclean hunger –
Of Irus and his scorn, or the legions Germanicus
Met, and was nearly scotted by whose anger,
I know, I realize, and am driven to pity
By unscorched eternal days of Babylon city
And any unsoothed restless greedy clamour,
As hunger for Empire, any use of war's hammer.
Tea and tobacco after decent labour
Would bring again England of pipe and tabor
Merry England again after four centuries,
Of dawn-rising and late-talking and go-as-you-please.

Thomas Hardy (1840–1928)

MEN WHO MARCH AWAY

SONG OF THE SOLDIERS

WHAT of the faith and fire within us
        Men who march away
Ere the barn-cocks say
Night is growing grey,
To hazards whence no tears can win us;
What of the faith and fire within us
Men who march away?

Is it a purblind prank, O think you,
Friend with the musing eye,
Who watch us stepping by,
With doubt and dolorous sigh?
Can much pondering so hoodwink you?
Is it a purblind prank, O think you,
Friend with the musing eye?

Nay. We see well what we are doing,
Though some may not see –
Dalliers as they be –
England's need are we;
Her distress would leave us rueing:
Nay. We well see what we are doing,
Though some may not see!

In our heart of hearts believing
Victory crowns the just,
And that braggarts must
Surely bite the dust,
Press we to the field ungrieving,
In our heart of hearts believing
Victory crowns the just.

Hence the faith and fire within us
Men who march away
Ere the barn-cocks say
Night is growing grey,
To hazards whence no tears can win us;
Hence the faith and fire within us
Men who march away.

CHANNEL FIRING

THAT night your great guns, unawares,
Shook all our coffins as we lay,
And broke the chancel window-squares,
We thought it was the Judgment-day

And sat upright. While drearisome
Arose the howl of wakened hounds:
The mouse let fall the altar-crumb,
The worms drew back into the mounds,

The glebe cow drooled. Till God called, 'No;
It's gunnery practice out at sea
Just as before you went below;
The world is as it used to be:

'All nations striving strong to make
Red war yet redder. Mad as hatters
They do no more for Christés sake
Than you who are helpless in such matters.

'That this is not the judgment-hour
For some of them's a blessed thing,
For if it were they'd have to scour
Hell's floor for so much threatening ....

'Ha, ha. It will be warmer when
I blow the trumpet (if indeed
I ever do; for you are men,
And rest eternal sorely need).'

So down we lay again. 'I wonder,
Will the world ever saner be,'
Said one, 'than when He sent us under
In our indifferent century!'

And many a skeleton shook his head.
'Instead of preaching forty year,'
My neighbour Parson Thirdly said,
'I wish I had stuck to pipes and beer.'

Again the guns disturbed the hour,
Roaring their readiness to avenge,
As far inland as Stourton Tower,
And Camelot, and starlit Stonehenge.

IN TIME OF 'THE BREAKING OF NATIONS'

I

Only a man harrowing clods
In a slow silent walk
With an old horse that stumbles and nods
Half asleep as they stalk.

II

Only thin smoke without flame
From the heaps of couch-grass;
Yet this will go onward the same
Though Dynasties pass.

III

Yonder a maid and her wight
Come whispering by:
War's annals will cloud into night
Ere their story die.

Teresa Hooley

A War Film

I SAW,
And with a catch of the breath and the heart's uplifting,
Sorrow and pride, the 'week's great draw' –
The Mons Retreat;
The 'Old Contemptibles' who fought, and died,
The horror and the anguish and the glory.

As in a dream,
Still hearing machine-guns rattle and shells scream,
I came out into the street.

When the day was done,
My little son
Wondered at bath-time why I kissed him so,
Naked upon my knee.
How could he know
The sudden terror that assaulted me? ...
The body I had borne
Nine moons beneath my heart,
A part of me...
If, someday,
It should be taken away
To War. Tortured. Torn.
Slain.
Rotting in No Man's Land, out in the rain –
My little son ...
Yet all those men had mothers, every one.

How should he know
Why I kissed and kissed and kissed him,

crooning his name?

He thought that I was daft.
He thought it was a game,
And laughed, and laughed.

A.E. Housman (1859–1936)

EPITAPH ON AN ARMY OF MERCENARIES

THESE, in the days when heaven was falling,
The hour when earth's foundations fled,
Followed their mercenary calling
And took their wages and are dead.

Their shoulders held the sky suspended;
They stood, and the earth's foundations stay;
What God abandoned, these defended,
And saved the sum of things for pay.

HERE DEAD WE LIE

HERE dead we lie because we did not choose
To live and shame the land from which we sprung.

Life, to be sure, is nothing much to lose;
But young men think it is, and we were young.

T.E. Hulme (1883–1917)

TRENCHES: ST ELOI

OVER the flat slope of St Eloi
   A wide wall of sandbags.
Night,
In the silence desultory men
Pottering over small fires, cleaning their mess-tins.
To and fro, from the lines,
Men walk as on Piccadilly,
Making paths in the dark,
Through scattered dead horses,
Over a dead Belgian's belly.

Philip Johnstone (J.S. Purvis, 1890–1968)

HIGH WOOD

LADIES and gentlemen, this is High Wood,
   Called by the French, Bois des Fourneaux,
The famous spot which in Nineteen-Sixteen,
July, August and September was the scene
Of long and bitterly contested strife,
By reason of its High commanding site.
Observe the effect of shell-fire in the trees
Standing and fallen; here is wire; this trench
For months inhabited, twelve times changed hands;
(They soon fall in), used later as a grave.
It has been said on good authority
That in the fighting for this patch of wood
Were killed somewhere above eight thousand men,
Of whom the greater part were buried here,

This mound on which you stand being ...
    Madame, please,
You are requested kindly not to touch
Or take away the Company's property
As souvenirs; you'll find we have on sale
A large variety, all guaranteed.
As I was saying, all is as it was,
This is an unknown British officer,
The tunic having lately rotted off.
Please follow me – this way ...
    the *path*, sir, *please*,
The ground which was secured at great expense
The Company keeps absolutely untouched,
And in that dug-out (genuine) we provide
Refreshments at a reasonable rate.
You are requested not to leave about
Paper, or ginger-beer bottles, or orange peel,
There are waste-paper baskets at the gate.

Rudyard Kipling (1865–1936)

FOR ALL WE HAVE AND ARE

For all we have and are,
    For all our children's fate,
Stand up and meet the war.
The Hun is at the gate!
Our world has passed away
In wantonness o'erthrown.
There is nothing left today
But steel and fire and stone.

Though all we knew depart,
The old commandments stand:
'In courage keep your heart,
In strength lift up your hand.'

Once more we hear the word
That sickened earth of old:
'No law except the sword
Unsheathed and uncontrolled,'
Once more it knits mankind,
Once more the nations go
To meet and break and bind
A crazed and driven foe.

Comfort, content, delight —
The ages' slow-bought gain —
They shrivelled in a night,
Only ourselves remain
To face the naked days
In silent fortitude,
Through perils and dismays
Renewd and re-renewed.

Though all we made depart,
The old commandments stand:
'In patience keep your heart,
In strength lift up your hand.'

No easy hopes or lies
Shall bring us to our goal,
But iron sacrifice
Of body, will, and soul.
There is but one task for all —
For each one life to give.
Who stands if freedom fall?
Who dies if England live?

My Boy Jack

' Have you news of my boy Jack?'
      Not this tide.
'When d'you think that he'll come back?'
Not with this wind blowing, and this tide.
'Has anyone else had word of him?'
Not this tide.
For what is sunk will hardly swim,
Not with this wind blowing and this tide.
'Oh, dear, what comfort can I find?'
None this tide,
Nor any tide,
Except he did not shame his kind –
Not even with that wind blowing, and that tide.
Then hold your head up all the more,
This tide,
And every tide;
Because he was the son you bore,
And gave to that wind blowing and that tide!

GETHSEMANE

1914–1918

THE Garden called Gethsemane
  In Picardy it was,
And there the people came to see
  The English soldiers pass.

We used to pass – we used to pass
  Or halt, as it might be,
And ship our masks in case of gas
  Beyond Gethsemane.

The Garden called Gethsemane,
  It held a pretty lass,
But all the time she talked to me
  I prayed my cup might pass.

The officer sat on the chair,
  The men lay on the grass,
And all the time we halted there
  I prayed my cup might pass.

It didn't pass – it didn't pass –
  It didn't pass from me.
I drank it when we met the gas
  Beyond Gethsemane.

COMMON FORM

IF any question why we died
Tell them, because our fathers lied.

A DEAD STATESMAN

I COULD not dig; I dared not rob;
Therefore I lied to please the mob.
Now all my lies are proved untrue
And I must face the men I slew.
What tale shall serve me here among
Mine angry and defrauded young?

Winifred M. Letts (1882–1971)

THE DESERTER

THERE was a man – don't mind his name,
Whom Fear had dogged by night and day.
He could not face the German guns
And so he turned and ran away.
Just that – he turned and ran away,
But who can judge him, you or I?
God makes a man of flesh and blood
Who yearns to live and not to die.
And this man when he feared to die
Was scared as any frightened child,
His knees were shaking under him,
His breath came fast, his eyes were wild.
I've seen a hare with eyes as wild,
With throbbing heart and sobbing breath.
But oh! it shames one's soul to see

A man in abject fear of death.
But fear had gripped him, so had death;
His number had gone up that day,
They might not heed his frightened eyes,
They shot him when the dawn was grey.
Blindfolded, when the dawn was grey,
He stood there in a place apart,
The shots rang out and down he fell,
An English bullet in his heart.
An English bullet in his heart!
But here's the irony of life —
His mother thinks he fought and fell
A hero, foremost in the strife.
So she goes proudly; to the strife
Her best, her hero son she gave.
O well for her she does not know
He lies in a deserter's grave.

W.S. Lyon (1893–1915)

I Tracked a Dead Man
Down a Trench

I TRACKED a dead man down a trench,
I knew not he was dead.
They told me he had gone that way,
And there his foot-marks led.

The trench was long and close and curved,
It seemed without an end;
And as I threaded each new bay
I thought to see my friend.

I went there stooping to the ground.
For, should I raise my head,
Death watched to spring; and how should then
A dead man find the dead?

At last I saw his back. He crouched
As still as still could be,
And when I called his name aloud
He did not answer me.

The floor-way of the trench was wet
Where he was crouching dead;
The water of the pool was brown,
And round him it was red.

I stole up softly where he stayed
With head hung down all slack,
And on his shoulders laid my hands
And drew him gently back.

And then, as I had guessed, I saw
His head, and how the crown –
I saw then why he crouched so still,
And why his head hung down.

Frederic Manning (1882–1935)

GROTESQUE

THESE are the damned circles Dante trod,
  Terrible in hopelessness,
But even skulls have their humour,
An eyeless and sardonic mockery:
And we,
Sitting with streaming eyes in the acrid smoke,
That murks our foul, damp billet,
Chant bitterly, with raucous voices
As a choir of frogs
In hideous irony, our patriotic songs.

William Orpen, 'Thiepval' (1917)

John McCrae (1872–1918)

IN FLANDERS FIELDS

IN Flanders fields the poppies blow
Between the crosses, row on row,
That mark our place; and in the sky
The larks, still bravely singing, fly
Scarce heard amid the guns below.

We are the Dead. Short days ago
We lived, felt dawn, saw sunset glow,
Loved and were loved, and now we lie
In Flanders fields.

Take up our quarrel with the foe:
To you from failing hands we throw
The torch; be yours to hold it high.
If ye break faith with us who die
We shall not sleep, though poppies grow
In Flanders fields.

Charlotte Mew (1869–1928)

THE CENOTAPH

NOT yet will those measureless fields be green again
Where only yesterday the wild sweet blood
                    of wonderful youth was shed;
There is a grave whose earth must hold too long,
                    too deep a stain,
Though for ever over it we may speak
                    as proudly as we may tread.

But here, where the watchers by lonely hearths from
    the thrust of an inward sword have more slowly bled,
We shall build the Cenotaph: Victory, winged,
        with Peace, winged too, at the column's head.
And over the stairway, at the foot – oh! here,
        leave desolate, passionate hands to spread
Violets, roses, and laurel, with the small, sweet,
           tinkling country things
Speaking so wistfully of other Springs,
From the little gardens of little places
      where son or sweetheart was born and bred.
In splendid sleep, with a thousand brothers
To lovers – to mothers
Here, too, lies he:
Under the purple, the green, the red,
It is all young life: it must break
        some women's hearts to see
Such a brave, gay coverlet to such a bed!
Only, when all is done and said,
God is not mocked and neither are the dead.
For this will stand in our Marketplace –
Who'll sell, who'll buy
(Will you or I
Lie each to each with the better grace)?
While looking into every busy whore's
        and huckster's face
As they drive their bargains, is the Face
Of God: and some young, piteous, murdered face.

'Saki' (H.H. Munro, 1870–1916)

CAROL

WHILE shepherds watched their flocks by night,
  All seated on the ground,
A high explosive shell came down,
And mutton rained around.

Sir Henry Newbolt (1862–1938)

CLIFTON CHAPEL

THIS is the Chapel: here, my son,
  Your father thought the thoughts of youth,
And heard the words that one by one
The touch of life has turned to truth.
Here in a day that is not far
You too may speak with noble ghosts
Of manhood and the vows of war
You made before the Lord of Hosts.

To set the cause above renown,
To love the game beyond the prize,
To honour, while you strike him down,
The foe that comes with fearless eyes;
To count the life of battle good,
And dear the land that gave you birth,
And dearer yet the brotherhood
That binds the brave of all the earth.

My son, the oath is yours: the end
Is His, who built the world for strife,
Who gave His children pain for friend,
And death for surest hope of life.
Today and here the fight's begun,
Of the great fellowship you're free;
Henceforth the school and you are one,
And what you are, the race shall be.

God send you fortune, yet be sure,
Among the lights that gleam and pass,
You'll live to follow none more pure
Than that which glows on yonder brass:
'*Qui procul hinc,*' the legend's writ, —
The frontier-grave is far away —
'*Qui ante diem periit:*
Sed miles, sed pro patria.'

A LETTER FROM THE FRONT

I WAS out early today, spying about
From the top of a haystack – such a lovely morning –
And when I mounted again to canter back
I saw across a field in the broad sunlight
A young Gunner Subaltern, stalking along
With a rook-rifle held at the read, and –
                              would you believe it? –
A domestic cat, soberly marching beside him.

So I laughed, and felt quite well disposed
                              to the youngster,
And shouted out 'the top of the morning' to him,
And wished him 'Good sport!' – and then I remembered
My rank, and his, and what I ought to be doing:
And I rode nearer, and added, 'I can only suppose
You have not seen the Commander-in-Chief's order
Forbidding English officers to annoy their Allies
By hunting and shooting.'
   But he stood and saluted
And said earnestly, 'I beg your pardon, Sir,
I was only going out to shoot a sparrow
To feed my cat with.'
   So there was the whole picture,
The lovely early morning, the occasional shell
Screeching and scattering past us, the empty landscape –
Empty, except for the young Gunner saluting,
And the cat, anxiously watching his every movement.

I may be wrong, or I may have told it badly,
But it struck me as being extremely ludicrous.

Robert Nichols (1893–1944)

FULFILMENT

Was there love once? I have forgotten her.
Was there grief once? Grief yet is mine.
Other loves I have, men rough, but men who stir
More grief, more joy, than love of thee and thine.

Faces cheerful, full of whimsical mirth,
Lined by the wind, burned by the sun;
Bodies enraptured by the abounding earth,
As whose children we are brethren: one.

And any moment may descend hot death
To shatter limbs! Pulp, tear, blast
Belovèd soldiers who love rough, life and breath
Not less for dying faithful to the last.

O the fading eyes, the grimed face turned bony,
Oped mouth gushing, fallen head,
Lessening pressure of a hand, shrunk,
                              clammed and stony!
O sudden spasm, release of the dead!

Was there love once? I have forgotten her.
Was there grief once? Grief yet is mine.
O loved, living, dying, heroic soldier,
All, all my joy, my grief, my love, are thine.

Wilfred Owen (1893–1918)

Strange Meeting

It seemed that out of the battle I escaped
Down some profound dull tunnel, long since scooped
Through granites which Titanic wars had groined.
Yet also there encumbered sleepers groaned,
Too fast in thought or death to be bestirred.
Then, as I probed them, one sprang up, and stared
With piteous recognition in fixed eyes,
Lifting distressful hands as if to bless.
And by his smile, I knew that sullen hall;
By his dead smile I knew we stood in Hell.
With a thousand fears that vision's face was grained;
Yet no blood reached there from the upper ground,
And no guns thumped, or down the flues made moan.
'Strange friend,' I said, 'Here is no cause to mourn.'
'None,' said the other, 'Save the undone years,
The hopelessness. Whatever hope is yours,
Was my life also; I went hunting wild
After the wildest beauty in the world,
Which lies not calm in eyes, or braided hair,
But mocks the steady running of the hour,
And if it grieves, grieves richlier than here.
For by my glee might many men have laughed,
And of my weeping something has been left,
Which must die now. I mean the truth untold,
The pity of war, the pity war distilled.
Now men will go content with what we spoiled.
Or, discontent, boil bloody, and be spilled.
They will be swift with swiftness of the tigress,

None will break ranks,
        though nations trek from progress.

Courage was mine, and I had mystery;
Wisdom was mine, and I had mastery;
To miss the march of this retreating world
Into vain citadels that are not walled.
Then, when much blood had clogged their chariot-wheels
I would go up and wash them from sweet wells,
Even with truths that lie too deep for taint.
I would have poured my spirit without stint
But not through wounds; not on the cess of war.
Foreheads of men have bled where no wounds were.
I am the enemy you killed, my friend.
I knew you in this dark; for so you frowned
Yesterday through me as you jabbed and killed.
I parried; but my hands were loath and cold.
Let us sleep now …'

APOLOGIA PRO POEMATE MEO

I, too, saw God through mud –
The mud that cracked on cheeks
        when wretches smiled.
  War brought more glory to their eyes than blood,
  And gave their laugh more glee than shakes a child.

Merry it was to laugh there –
  Where death becomes absurd and life absurder.
  For power was on us as we slashed bones bare
  Not to feel sickness or remorse of murder.

I, too, have dropped off fear –
  Behind the barrage, dead as my platoon,

And sailed my spirit surging, light and clear
Past the entanglement where hopes lay strewn;

And witnessed exultation –
Faces that used to curse me, scowl for scowl,
Shine and lift up with passion of oblation,
Seraphic for an hour; though they were foul.

I have made fellowships –
Untold of happy lovers in old song.
For love is not the binding of fair lips
With the soft silk of eyes that look and long,

By Joy, whose ribbon slips –
But wound with war's hard wire
                                  whose stakes are strong;
Bound with the bandage of the arm that drips;
Knit in the welding of the rifle-thong.

I have perceived much beauty
In the hoarse oaths that kept our courage straight;
Heard music in the silentness of duty;
Found peace where shell-storms
                                  spouted reddest spate.

Nevertheless, except you share
With them in hell the sorrowful dark of hell,
Whose world is but the trembling of a flare,
And heaven but as the highway for a shell,

You shall not hear their mirth:
You shall not come to think them well content
By any jest of mine. These men are worth
Your tears. You are not worth their merriment.

John Singer Sargent, 'Street in Arras' (1918)

THE SHOW

We have fallen in the dreams the ever-living
Breathe on the tarnished mirror of the world,
And then smooth out with ivory hands and sigh

W.B. Yeats

M Y soul looked down
             from a vague height with Death,
As unremembering how I rose or why,
And saw a sad land, weak with sweats of dearth,
Gray, cratered like the moon with hollow woe,
And pitted with great pocks and scabs of plagues.

Across its beard, that horror of harsh wire,
There moved thin caterpillars, slowly uncoiled.
It seemed they pushed themselves to be as plugs
Of ditches, where they writhed and shrivelled, killed.

By them had slimy paths been trailed and scraped
Round myriad warts that might be little hills.

From gloom's last dregs
                  these long-strung creatures crept,
And vanished out of dawn down hidden holes.

(And smell came up from those foul openings
As out of mouths, or deep wounds deepening.)

On dithering feet upgathered, more and more,
Brown strings towards strings of gray,
                                with bristling spines,
All migrants from green fields, intent on mire.

Those that were grey, of more abundant spawns,

Ramped on the rest and ate them and were eaten.

I saw their bitten backs curve, loop, and straighten,
I watched those agonies curl, lift, and flatten.

Whereat, in terror what that sight might mean,
I reeled and shivered earthward like a feather.

And Death fell with me, like a deepening moan.
And He, picking a manner of worm, which half had hid
Its bruises in the earth, but crawled no further,
Showed me its feet, the feet of many men,
And the fresh-severed head of it, my head.

PARABLE OF THE OLD MAN
AND THE YOUNG

So Abram rose, and clave the wood, and went,
And took the fire with him, and a knife.
And as they sojourned both of them together,
Isaac the first-born spake and said, My Father,
Behold the preparations, fire and iron,
But where the lamb for this burnt-offering?
Then Abram bound the youth with belts and straps,
And builded parapets and trenches there,
And stretched forth the knife to slay his son.
When lo! an angel called him out of heaven,
Saying, Lay not thy hand upon the lad,
Neither do anything to him, thy son. Behold,
A ram caught in a thicket by its horns;
Offer the Ram of Pride instead of him.
But the old man would not so, but slew his son,
And half the seed of Europe, one by one.

MENTAL CASES

WHO are these? Why sit they here in twilight?
  Wherefore rock they, purgatorial shadows,
Drooping tongues from jaws that slob their relish,
Baring teeth that leer like skulls' tongues wicked?
Stroke on stroke of pain – but what slow panic,
Gouged these chasms round their fretted sockets?
Ever from their hair and through their hands' palms
Misery swelters. Surely we have perished
Sleeping, and walk hell; but who these hellish?

– These are men whose minds the Dead have ravished.
Memory fingers in their hair of murders,
Multitudinous murders they once witnessed.
Wading sloughs of flesh these helpless wander,
Treading blood from lungs that had loved laughter.
Always they must see these things and hear them,
Batter of guns and shatter of flying muscles,
Carnage incomparable and human squander,
Rucked too thick for these men's extrication.

Therefore still their eyeballs shrink tormented
Back into their brains, because on their sense
Sunlight seems a blood-smear; night comes blood-black;
Dawn breaks open like a wound that bleeds afresh.
– Thus their heads wear this hilarious, hideous,
Awful falseness of set-smiling corpses.
– Thus their hands are plucking at each other;
Picking at the rope-knouts of their scourging;
Snatching after us who smote them, brother,
Pawing us who dealt them war and madness.

ANTHEM FOR DOOMED YOUTH

WHAT passing-bells for these who die as cattle?
    Only the monstrous anger of the guns.
  Only the stuttering rifles' rapid rattle
Can patter out their hasty orisons.
No mockeries for them; no prayers nor bells,
Nor any voice of mourning save the choirs, –
The shrill, demented choirs of wailing shells;
And bugles calling for them from sad shires.

What candles may be held to speed them all?
    Not in the hands of boys, but in their eyes
Shall shine the holy glimmers of goodbyes.
    The pallor of girls' brows shall be their pall;
Their flowers the tenderness of patient minds,
And each slow dusk a drawing-down of blinds.

THE SEND-OFF

DOWN the close, darkening lanes they sang their way
    To the siding-shed,
And lined the train with faces grimly gay.

Their breasts were stuck all white with wreath and spray
As men's are, dead.

Dull porters watched them, and a casual tramp
Stood staring hard,
Sorry to miss them from the upland camp.
Then, unmoved, signals nodded, and a lamp
Winked to the guard.

So secretly, like wrongs hushed-up, they went.
They were not ours:
We never heard to which front these were sent.

Nor there if they yet mock what women meant
Who gave them flowers.

Shall they return to beatings of great bells
In wild trainloads?
A few, a few, too few for drums and yells,
May creep back, silent, to still village wells
Up half-known roads.

INSENSIBILITY

I

HAPPY are men who yet before they are killed
Can let their veins run cold.
Whom no compassion fleers
Or makes their feet
Sore on the alleys cobbled with their brothers.
The front line withers,
But they are troops who fade, not flowers
For poets' tearful fooling:
Men, gaps for filling:
Losses who might have fought
Longer; but no one bothers.

II

And some cease feeling
Even themselves or for themselves.
Dullness best solves
The tease and doubt of shelling,
And Chance's strange arithmetic
Comes simpler than the reckoning of their shilling.
They keep no check on Armies' decimation.

III

Happy are these who lose imagination:
They have enough to carry with ammunition.
Their spirit drags no pack,
Their old wounds save with cold can not more ache.
Having seen all things red,
Their eyes are rid
Of the hurt of the colour of blood for ever.
And terror's first constriction over,
Their hearts remain small drawn.
Their senses in some scorching cautery of battle
Now long since ironed,
Can laugh among the dying, unconcerned.

IV

Happy the soldier home, with not a notion
How somewhere, every dawn, some men attack,
And many sighs are drained.
Happy the lad whose mind was never trained:
His days are worth forgetting more than not.
He sings along the march
Which we march taciturn, because of dusk,
The long, forlorn, relentless trend
From larger day to huger night.

V

We wise, who with a thought besmirch
Blood over all our soul,
How should we see our task
But through his blunt and lashless eyes?
Alive, he is not vital overmuch;
Dying, not mortal overmuch;
Nor sad, nor proud,
Nor curious at all.
He cannot tell
Old men's placidity from his.

VI

But cursed are dullards whom no cannon stuns,
That they should be as stones.
Wretched are they, and mean
With paucity that never was simplicity.
By choice they made themselves immune
To pity and whatever mourns in man
Before the last sea and the hapless stars;
Whatever mourns when many leave these shores;
Whatever shares
The eternal reciprocity of tears.

John Singer Sargent, 'Gassed' (c. 1918)

DULCE ET DECORUM EST

Bent double, like old beggars under sacks,
Knock-kneed, coughing like hags,
                                    we cursed through sludge,
Till on the haunting flares we turned our backs,
And towards our distant rest began to trudge.
Men marched asleep. Many had lost their boots,
But limped on, blood-shod. All went lame, all blind;
Drunk with fatigue; deaf even to the hoots
Of gas-shells dropping softly behind.

Gas! GAS! Quick, boys! – An ecstasy of fumbling,
Fitting the clumsy helmets just in time,
But someone still was yelling out and stumbling
And flound'ring like a man in fire or lime. –
Dim through the misty panes and thick green light,
As under a green sea, I saw him drowning.

In all my dreams before my helpless sight
He plunges at me, guttering, choking, drowning.

If in some smothering dreams, you too could pace
Behind the wagon that we flung him in,
And watch the white eyes writhing in his face,
His hanging face, like a devil's sick of sin;
If you could hear, at every jolt, the blood
Come gargling from the froth-corrupted lungs,
Bitter as the cud
Of vile, incurable sores on innocent tongues, –
My friend, you would not tell with such high zest
To children ardent for some desperate glory,
The old Lie: *Dulce et decorum est*
Pro patria mori.

THE SENTRY

WE'D found an old Boche dug-out, and he knew,
   And gave us hell, for shell on frantic shell
Hammered on top, but never quite burst through.
Rain, guttering down in waterfalls of slime
Kept slush waist high, that rising hour by hour,
Choked up the steps too thick with clay to climb.
What murk of air remained stank old, and sour
With fumes of whizz-bangs, and the smell of men
Who'd lived there years, and left their curse in the den,
If not their corpses. …
                    There we herded from the blast
Of whizz-bangs, but one found our door at last.
Buffeting eyes and breath, snuffing the candles.
And thud! flump! thud!
                    down the steep steps came thumping
And splashing in the flood, deluging muck –
The sentry's body; then his rifle, handles
Of old Boche bombs, and mud in ruck on ruck.
We dredged him up, for killed, until he whined
'O sir, my eyes – I'm blind – I'm blind, I'm blind!'
Coaxing, I held a flame against his lids
And said if he could see the least blurred light
He was not blind; in time he'd get all right.
'I can't,' he sobbed. Eyeballs, huge-bulged like squids'
Watch my dreams still; but I forgot him there
In posting next for duty, and sending a scout
To beg a stretcher somewhere, and floundering about
To other posts under the shrieking air.

Those other wretches, how they bled and spewed,
And one who would have drowned himself for good, –
I try not to remember these things now.
Let dread hark back for one word only: how
Half-listening to that sentry's moans and jumps,
And the wild chattering of his broken teeth,
Renewed most horribly whenever crumps
Pummelled the roof and slogged the air beneath –
Through the dense din, I say, we heard him shout
'I see your lights!' But ours had long died out.

FUTILITY

Move him into the sun –
Gently its touch awoke him once,
At home, whispering of fields unsown.
Always it woke him, even in France,
Until this morning and this snow.
If anything might rouse him now
The kind old sun will know.

Think how it wakes the seeds –
Woke, once, the clays of a cold star.
Are limbs so dear-achieved, are sides
Full-nerved – still warm – too hard to stir?
Was it for this the clay grew tall?
– O what made fatuous sunbeams toil
To break earth's sleep at all?

THE DEAD-BEAT

HE dropped – more sullenly than wearily,
Lay stupid like a cod, heavy like meat,
And none of us could kick him to his feet;
Just blinked at my revolver, blearily;
– Didn't appear to know a war was on,
Or see the blasted trench at which he stared.
'I'll do 'em in,' he whined, 'If this hand's spared,
I'll murder them, I will.'
                    A low voice said,
'It's Blighty, p'raps, he sees; his pluck's all gone,
Dreaming of all the valiant, that aren't dead:
Bold uncles, smiling ministerially;
Maybe his brave young wife, getting her fun
In some new home, improved materially.
It's not these stiffs have crazed him; nor the Hun.'

We sent him down at last, out of the way.
Unwounded – stout lad, too, before that strafe.
Malingering? Stretcher-bearers winked, 'Not half!'

Next day I heard the Doc's well-whiskied laugh:
'That scum you sent last night soon died. Hooray!'

Félix Vallotton, 'Le Cimetière de Châlons-sur-Marne'
('The Cemetery of Châlons-sur-Marne') (1917)

EXPOSURE

I

O<small>UR</small> brains ache, in the merciless iced east winds
                                that knife us ...
Wearied we keep awake because the night is silent ...
Low drooping flares confuse our memory
                                of the salient ...
Worried by silence, sentries whisper, curious, nervous,
    But nothing happens.

Watching, we hear the mad gusts tugging on the wire,
Like twitching agonies of men among its brambles.
Northward, incessantly, the flickering gunnery rumbles,
Far off, like a dull rumour of some other war.
    What are we doing here?

The poignant misery of dawn begins to grow ...
We only know war lasts, rain soaks,
                                and clouds sag stormy.
Dawn massing in the east her melancholy army
Attacks once more in ranks on shivering ranks of grey,
    But nothing happens.

Sudden successive flights of bullets streak the silence.
Less deadly than the air that shudders black with snow,
With sidelong flowing flakes that flock, pause and renew,
We watch them wandering up and down
                                the wind's nonchalance,
    But nothing happens.

II

Pale flakes with lingering stealth come
                              feeling for our faces –
We cringe in holes, back on forgotten dreams,
                              and stare, snow-dazed,
Deep into grassier ditches. So we drowse, sun-dozed,
Littered with blossoms trickling
                              where the blackbird fusses.
    Is it that we are dying?

Slowly our ghosts drag home:
                              glimpsing the sunk fires, glozed
With crusted dark-red jewels; crickets jingle there;
For hours the innocent mice rejoice: the house is theirs;
Shutters and doors all closed:
                              on us the doors are closed –
    We turn back to our dying.

Since we believe not otherwise can kind fires burn;
Nor ever suns smile true on child, or field, or fruit.
For God's invincible spring our love is made afraid;
Therefore, not loath, we lie out here;
                              therefore were born,
    For love of God seems dying.

Tonight, His frost will fasten on this mud and us,
Shrivelling many hands and puckering foreheads crisp.
The burying-party, picks and shovels
                              in their shaking grasp,
Pause over half-known faces. All their eyes are ice,
    But nothing happens.

SPRING OFFENSIVE

HALTED against the shade of a last hill,
They fed, and, lying easy, were at ease
And, finding comfortable chests and knees
Carelessly slept. But many there stood still
To face the stark, blank sky beyond the ridge,
Knowing their feet had come to the end of the world.

Marvelling they stood, and watched
       the long grass swirled
By the May breeze, murmurous with wasp and midge,
For though the summer oozed into their veins
Like the injected drug for their bodies' pains,
Sharp on their souls hung the imminent line of grass,
Fearfully flashed the sky's mysterious glass.

Hour after hour they ponder the warm field –
And the far valley behind, where the buttercups
Had blessed with gold their slow boots coming up,
Where even the little brambles would not yield,
But clutched and clung to them like sorrowing hands;
They breathe like trees unstirred.

Till like a cold gust thrills the little word
At which each body and its soul begird
And tighten them for battle. No alarms
Of bugles, no high flags, no clamorous haste –
Only a lift and flare of eyes that faced
The sun, like a friend with whom their love is done.
O larger shone that smile against the sun –
Mightier than his whose bounty these have spurned.

So, soon they topped the hill, and raced together
Over an open stretch of herb and heather
Exposed. And instantly the whole sky burned
With fury against them; and soft sudden cups
Opened in thousands for their blood;
                            and the green slopes
Chasmed and steepened sheer to infinite space.

Of them who running on that last high place
Leapt to swift unseen bullets, or went up
On the hot blast and fury of hell's upsurge,
Or plunged and fell away past this world's verge,
Some say God caught them even before they fell.

But what say such as from existence' brink
Ventured but drave too swift to sink,
The few who rushed in the body to enter hell,
And there out-fiending all its fiends and flames
With superhuman inhumanities,
Long-famous glories, immemorial shames –
And crawling slowly back, have by degrees
Regained cool peaceful air in wonder –
Why speak they not of comrades that went under?

THE CHANCES

I MIND as 'ow the night afore that show
Us five got talking, – we was in the know.
'Over the top tomorrer; boys, we're for it.
First wave we are, first ruddy wave; that's tore it.'
'Ah well,' says Jimmy, – an' 'e's seen some scrappin' –
'There ain't no more nor five things as can 'appen:
Ye get knocked out; else wounded – bad or cushy;
Scuppered; or nowt except yer feeling mushy.'

One of us got the knock-out, blown to chops.
T'other was hurt, like, losin' both 'is props.
An' one, to use the word of 'ypocrites,
'Ad the misfortoon to be took by Fritz.
Now me, I wasn't scratched, praise God Almighty
(Though next time please I'll thank 'im for a blighty),
But poor young Jim, 'e's livin' an' 'e's not;
'E reckoned 'e'd five chances, an' 'e 'ad;
'E's wounded, killed, and pris'ner, all the lot –
The ruddy lot all rolled in one. Jim's mad.

Smile, Smile, Smile

Head to limp head, the sunk-eyed wounded scanned
Yesterday's *Mail*; the casualties (typed small)
And (large) Vast Booty from our Latest Haul.
Also, they read of Cheap Homes, not yet planned
For, said the paper, 'When this war is done
The men's first instinct will be making homes.
Meanwhile their foremost need is aerodromes,
It being certain war has just begun.
Peace would do wrong to our undying dead, –
The sons we offered might regret they died
If we got nothing lasting in their stead.
We must be solidly indemnified.
Though all be worthy Victory which all bought,
We rulers sitting in this ancient spot
Would wrong our very selves if we forgot
The greatest glory will be theirs who fought,
Who kept this nation in integrity.'
Nation? – The half-limbed readers did not chafe
But smiled at one another curiously
Like secret men who know their secret safe.
(This is the thing they know and never speak,
That England one by one had fled to France,
Not many elsewhere now save under France.)
Pictures of these broad smiles appear each week,
And people in whose voice real feeling rings
Say: How they smile! They're happy now, poor things.

A TERRE

BEING THE PHILOSOPHY OF MANY SOLDIERS

Sit on the bed; I'm blind, and three parts shell.
Be careful; can't shake hands now; never shall.
Both arms have mutinied against me – brutes.
My fingers fidget like ten idle brats.

I tried to peg out soldierly – no use!
One dies of war like any old disease.
This bandage feels like pennies on my eyes.
I have my medals? – Discs to make eyes close.
My glorious ribbons? – Ripped from my own back
In scarlet shreds. (That's for your poetry book.)

A short life and a merry one, my buck!
We used to say we'd hate to live dead old –
Yet now ... I'd willingly be puffy, bald,
And patriotic. Buffers catch from boys
At least the jokes hurled at them. I suppose
Little I'd ever teach a son, but hitting,
Shooting, war, hunting, all the arts of hurting.
Well, that's what I learnt – that, and making money.

Your fifty years ahead seem none too many?
Tell me how long I've got? God! For one year
To help myself to nothing more than air!
One Spring! Is one too good to spare, too long?
Spring wind would work its own way to my lung,
And grow me legs as quick as lilac-shoots.

My servant's lamed, but listen how he shouts!
When I'm lugged out, he'll still be good for that.
Here in this mummy-case, you know, I've thought
How well I might have swept his floors for ever.
I'd ask no night off when the bustle's over,
Enjoying so the dirt. Who's prejudiced
Against a grimed hand when his own's quite dust,
Less live than specks that in the sun-shafts turn,
Less warm than dust that mixes with arms' tan?
I'd love to be a sweep, now, black as Town,
Yes, or a muckman. Must I be his load?

O Life, Life, let me breathe – a dug-out rat!
Not worse than ours the existences rats lead –
Nosing along at night down some safe vat,
They find a shell-proof home before they rot.
Dead men may envy living mites in cheese,
Or good germs even. Microbes have their joys,
And subdivide, and never come to death.
Certainly flowers have the easiest time on earth.
'I shall be one with nature, herb, and stone.'
Shelley would tell me. Shelley would be stunned:
The dullest Tommy hugs that fancy now.
'Pushing up daisies,' is their creed, you know.

To grain, then, go my fat, to buds my sap,
For all the usefulness there is in soap.
D'you think the Boche will ever stew man-soup?
Some day, no doubt, if ...
    Friend, be very sure
I shall be better off with plants that share
More peaceably the meadow and the shower.
Soft rains will touch me – as they could touch once,
And nothing but the sun shall make me ware.
Your guns may crash around me. I'll not hear;
Or, if I wince, I shall not know I wince.

Don't take my soul's poor comfort for your jest.
Soldiers may grow a soul when turned to fronds,
But here the thing's best left at home with friends.

My soul's a little grief, grappling your chest,
To climb your throat on sobs; easily chased
On other sighs and wiped by fresher winds.

Carry my crying spirit till it's weaned
To do without what blood remained these wounds.

William Orpen, 'The Receiving Room:
the 42nd Stationary Hospital'

DISABLED

HE sat in a wheeled chair, waiting for dark,
　　And shivered in his ghastly suit of grey,
Legless, sewn short at elbow. Through the park
Voices of boys rang saddening like a hymn,
Voices of play and pleasure after day,
Till gathering sleep had mothered them from him.

About this time Town used to swing so gay
When glow-lamps budded in the light-blue trees,
And girls glanced lovelier as the air grew dim –
In the old times, before he threw away his knees.
Now he will never feel again how slim
Girls' waists are, or how warm their subtle hands;
All of them touch him like some queer disease.

There was an artist silly for his face,
For it was younger than his youth, last year.
Now he is old; his back will never brace;
He's lost his colour very far from here,
Poured it down shell-holes till the veins ran dry,
And half his lifetime lapsed in the hot race,
And leap of purple spurted from his thigh.

One time he liked a blood-smear down his leg,
After the matches, carried shoulder-high.
It was after football, when he'd drunk a peg,
He thought he'd better join. He wonders why . . .
Someone had said he'd look a god in kilts,
That's why; and maybe, too, to please his Meg;
Aye, that was it, to please the giddy jilts
He asked to join. He didn't have to beg;

Smiling they wrote his lie; aged nineteen years.
Germans he scarcely thought of; all their guilt,
And Austria's, did not move him. And no fears
Of Fear came yet. He thought of jewelled hilts
For daggers in plaid socks; of smart salutes;
And care of arms; and leave; and pay arrears;
Esprit de corps; and hints for young recruits.
And soon he was drafted out with drums and cheers.

Some cheered him home, but not as crowds cheer Goal.
Only a solemn man who brought him fruits
Thanked him; and then inquired about his soul.

Now, he will spend a few sick years in Institutes,
And do what things the rules consider wise,
And take whatever pity they may dole.
Tonight he noticed how the women's eyes
Passed from him to the strong men that were whole.
How cold and late it is! Why don't they come
And put him into bed? Why don't they come?

MINERS

THERE was a whispering in my hearth,
    A sigh of the coal,
Grown wistful of a former earth
It might recall.

I listened for a tale of leaves
And smothered ferns;
Frond-forests; and the low, sly lives
Before the fawns.

My fire might show steam-phantoms simmer
From Time's old cauldron,
Before the birds made nests in summer,
Or men had children.

But the coals were murmuring of their mine,
And moans down there
Of boys that slept wry sleep, and men
Writhing for air.

And I saw white bones in the cinder-shard.
Bones without number;
For many hearts with coal are charred,
And few remember.

I thought of all who worked dark pits
Of war, and died
Digging the rock where Death reputes
Peace lies indeed.

Comforted years will sit soft-chaired
In rooms of amber;
The years will stretch their hands, well-cheered
By our lives' ember.

The centuries will burn rich loads
With which we groaned,
Whose warmth shall lull their dreaming lids
While songs are crooned.
But they will not dream of us poor lads
Left in the ground.

An Imperial Elegy

Not one corner of a foreign field
But a span as wide as Europe;
An appearance of a titan's grave,
And the length thereof a thousand miles,
It crossed all Europe like a mystic road,
Or as the Spirits' pathway lieth on the night.
And I heard a voice crying
This is the Path of Glory.

INSPECTION

'You! What d'you mean by this?' I rapped.
    'You dare come on parade like this?'
'Please, sir, it's –' ''Old yer mouth,'
                                    the sergeant snapped.
'I takes 'is name, sir?' – 'Please, and then dismiss.'

Some days 'confined to camp' he got,
For being 'dirty on parade'.
He told me, afterwards, the damnèd spot
Was blood, his own. 'Well, blood is dirt,' I said.

'Blood's dirt,' he laughed, looking away,
Far off to where his wound had bled
And almost merged for ever into clay.
'The world is washing out its stains,' he said.
'It doesn't like our cheeks so red:
Young blood's its great objection.
But when we're duly white-washed, being dead,
The race will bear Field-Marshal God's inspection.'

THE LETTER

WITH B.E.F. June 10. Dear Wife,
    (Oh blast this pencil. 'Ere, Bill, lend's a knife.)
I'm in the pink at present, dear.
I think the war will end this year.
We don't see much of them square-'eaded 'Uns.
We're out of harm's way, not bad fed.
I'm longing for a taste of your old buns.
(Say, Jimmie, spare's a bite of bread.)
There don't seem much to say just now.
(Yer what? Then don't, yer ruddy cow!
And give us back me cigarette!)
I'll soon be 'ome. You mustn't fret.
My feet's improvin', as I told you of.
We're out in rest now. Never fear.
(VRACH! By crumbs, but that was near.)
Mother might spare you half a sov.
Kiss Nell and Bert. When me and you –
(Eh? What the 'ell! Stand to? Stand to!
Jim, give's a hand with pack on, lad.
Guh! Christ! I'm hit. Take 'old. Aye, bad.
No, damn your iodine. Jim? 'Ere!
Write my old girl, Jim, there's a dear.)

Félix Vallotton, 'Les Barbelés' ('Barbed Wire') (1916)

Edgell Rickword (1898–1982)

TRENCH POETS

I KNEW a man, he was my chum,
but he grew blacker every day,
and would not brush the flies away,
nor blanch however fierce the hum
of passing shells; I used to read,
to rouse him, random things from Donne –
like 'Get with child a mandrake-root.'
But you can tell he was far gone,
for he lay gaping, mackerel-eyed,
and stiff, and senseless as a post
even when that old poet cried
'I long to talk with some old lover's ghost.'

I tried the Elegies one day,
But he, because he heard me say:
'What needst thou have no more covering than a man?'
grinned nastily, and so I knew
the worms had got his brains at last.
There was one thing that I might do
to starve the worms; I racked my head
for healthy things and quoted Maud.
His grin got worse and I could see
he sneered at passion's purity.
He stank so badly, though we were great chums
I had to leave him; then rats ate his thumbs.

Isaac Rosenberg (1890–1918)

ON RECEIVING NEWS OF THE WAR

SNOW is a strange white word.
No ice or frost
Has asked of bud or bird
For Winter's cost.

Yet ice and frost and snow
From earth to sky
This Summer land doth know.
No man knows why.

In all men's hearts it is.
Some spirit old
Hath turned with malign kiss
Our lives to mould.

Red fangs have torn His face.
God's blood is shed.
He mourns from His lone place
His children dead.

O! ancient crimson curse!
Corrode, consume.
Give back this universe
Its pristine bloom.

BREAK OF DAY IN THE TRENCHES

THE darkness crumbles away.
　It is the same old druid Time as ever,
Only a live thing leaps my hand,
A queer sardonic rat,
As I pull the parapet's poppy
To stick behind my ear.
Droll rat, they would shoot you if they knew
Your cosmopolitan sympathies.
Now you have touched this English hand
You will do the same to a German
Soon, no doubt, if it be your pleasure
To cross the sleeping green between.
It seems you inwardly grin as you pass
Strong eyes, fine limbs, haughty athletes,
Less chanced than you for life,
Bonds to the whims of murder,
Sprawled in the bowels of the earth,
The torn fields of France.
What do you see in our eyes
At the shrieking iron and flame
Hurled through still heavens?
What quaver – what heart aghast?
Poppies whose roots are in men's veins
Drop, and are ever dropping;
But mine in my ear is safe,
Just a little white with the dust.

DEAD MAN'S DUMP

THE plunging limbers over the shattered track
Racketed with their rusty freight,
Stuck out like many crowns of thorns,
And the rusty stakes like sceptres old
To stay the flood of brutish men
Upon our brothers dear.

The wheels lurched over sprawled dead
But pained them not, though their bones crunched,
Their shut mouths made no moan.
They lie there huddled, friend and foeman,
Man born of man, and born of woman,
And shells go crying over them
From night till night and now.

Earth has waited for them,
All the time of their growth
Fretting for their decay:
Now she has them at last!
In the strength of their strength
Suspended – stopped and held.

What fierce imaginings their dark souls lit?
Earth! have they gone into you!
Somewhere they must have gone,
And flung on your hard back
Is their soul's sack
Emptied of God-ancestralled essences.
Who hurled them out? Who hurled?

None saw their spirits' shadow shake the grass,
Or stood aside for the half used life to pass
Out of those doomed nostrils and the doomed mouth,
When the swift iron burning bee
Drained the wild honey of their youth.

What of us who, flung on the shrieking pyre,
Walk, our usual thoughts untouched,
Our lucky limbs as on ichor fed,
Immortal seeming ever?
Perhaps when the flames beat loud on us,
A fear may choke in our veins
And the startled blood may stop.

The air is loud with death,
The dark air spurts with fire,
The explosions ceaseless are.
Timelessly now, some minutes past,
Those dead strode time with vigorous life,
Till the shrapnel called 'An end!'
But not to all. In bleeding pangs
Some borne on stretchers dreamed of home,
Dear things, war-blotted from their hearts.

Maniac Earth! howling and flying, your bowel
Seared by the jagged fire, the iron love,
The impetuous storm of savage love.
Dark Earth! dark Heavens! swinging in chemic smoke,
What dead are born when you kiss each soundless soul
With lightning and thunder from your mined heart,
Which man's self dug, and his blind fingers loosed?

A man's brains splattered on
A stretcher-bearer's face;
His shook shoulders slipped their load,
But when they bent to look again
The drowning soul was sunk too deep
For human tenderness.

They left this dead with the older dead,
Stretched at the crossroads.

Burnt black by strange decay
Their sinister faces lie,
The lid over each eye,
The grass and coloured clay
More motion have than they,
Joined to the great sunk silences.

Here is one not long dead;
His dark hearing caught our far wheels,
And the choked soul stretched weak hands
To reach the living word the far wheels said,
The blood-dazed intelligence beating for light,
Crying through the suspense of the far torturing wheels
Swift for the end to break
Or the wheels to break,
Cried as the tide of the world broke over his sight.

Will they come? Will they ever come?
Even as the mixed hoofs of the mules,
The quivering-bellied mules,
And the rushing wheels all mixed
With his tortured upturned sight.
So we crashed round the bend,
We heard his weak scream,
We heard his very last sound,
And our wheels grazed his dead face.

IN THE TRENCHES

I SNATCHED two poppies
From the parapet's ledge,
Two bright red poppies
That winked on the ledge.
Behind my ear
I stuck one through,
One blood red poppy
I gave to you.

The sandbags narrowed
And screwed out our jest,
And tore the poppy
You had on your breast ...
Down – a shell – O! Christ,
I am choked ... safe ... dust blind, I
See trench floor poppies
Strewn. Smashed you lie.

William Orpen, 'The Somme: A Clear Day'

LOUSE HUNTING

NUDES – stark and glistening,
Yelling in lurid glee. Grinning faces
And raging limbs
Whirl over the floor one fire.
For a shirt verminously busy
Yon soldier tore from his throat, with oaths
Godhead might shrink at, but not the lice.
And soon the shirt was aflare
Over the candle he'd lit while we lay.

Then we all sprang up and stript
To hunt the verminous brood.
Soon like a demons' pantomime
The place was raging.
See the silhouettes agape,
See the gibbering shadows
Mixed with the battled arms on the wall.
See gargantuan hooked fingers
Pluck in supreme flesh
To smutch supreme littleness.
See the merry limbs in hot Highland fling
Because some wizard vermin
Charmed from the quiet this revel
When our ears were half lulled
By the dark music
Blown from Sleep's trumpet.

RETURNING, WE HEAR THE LARKS

SOMBRE the night is.
And though we have our lives, we know
What sinister threat lies there.

Dragging these anguished limbs, we only know
This poison-blasted track opens on our camp –
On a little safe sleep.

But hark! joy – joy – strange joy.
Lo! heights of night ringing with unseen larks.
Music showering our upturned list'ning faces.

Death could drop from the dark
As easily as song –
But song only dropped,
Like a blind man's dreams on the sand
By dangerous tides,
Like a girl's dark hair for she dreams no ruin lies there,
Or her kisses where a serpent hides.

THE IMMORTALS

I KILLED them, but they would not die.
Yea! all the day and all the night
For them I could not rest or sleep,
Nor guard from them nor hide in flight.

Then in my agony I turned
And made my hands red in their gore.
In vain – for faster than I slew
They rose more cruel than before.

I killed and killed with slaughter mad;
I killed till all my strength was gone.
And still they rose to torture me,
For Devils only die in fun.

I used to think the Devil hid
In women's smiles and wine's carouse.
I called him Satan, Beelzebub.
But now I call him dirty louse.

Siegfried Sassoon (1886–1967)

'THEY'

THE Bishop tells us: 'When the boys come back
'They will not be the same; for they'll have fought
'In a just cause: they lead the last attack
'On Anti-Christ; their comrades' blood has bought
'New right to breed an honourable race.
'They have challenged Death and dared him face to face.'

'We're none of us the same!' the boys reply.
'For George lost both his legs; and Bill's stone blind;
'Poor Jim's shot through the lungs and like to die;
'And Bert's gone syphilitic: you'll not find
'A chap who's served that hasn't found some change.'
And the Bishop said: 'The ways of God are strange!'

A SUBALTERN

HE turned to me with his kind, sleepy gaze
And fresh face slowly brightening to the grin
That sets my memory back to summer days,
With twenty runs to make, and last man in.
He told me he'd been having a bloody time
In trenches, crouching for the crumps to burst,
While squeaking rats scampered across the slime
And the grey palsied weather did its worst.
But as he stamped and shivered in the rain,
My stale philosophies had served him well;
Dreaming about his girl had sent his brain
Blanker than ever – she'd no place in Hell. ...
'Good God!' he laughed, and slowly filled his pipe,
Wondering 'why he always talked such tripe'.

DREAMERS

SOLDIERS are citizens of death's grey land,
Drawing no dividend from time's tomorrows.
In the great hour of destiny they stand,
Each with his feuds, and jealousies, and sorrows.
Soldiers are sworn to action; they must win
Some flaming, fatal climax with their lives.
Soldiers are dreamers; when the guns begin
They think of firelit homes, clean beds, and wives.

I see them in foul dug-outs, gnawed by rats,
And in the ruined trenches, lashed with rain,
Dreaming of things they did with balls and bats,
And mocked by hopeless longing to regain
Bank-holidays, and picture shows, and spats,
And going to the office in the train.

THE DEATH-BED

H E drowsed and was aware of silence heaped
Round him, unshaken as the steadfast walls;
Aqueous like floating rays of amber light,
Soaring and quivering in the wings of sleep.
Silence and safety; and his mortal shore
Lipped by the inward, moonless waves of death.

Someone was holding water to his mouth.
He swallowed, unresisting; moaned and dropped
Through crimson gloom to darkness; and forgot
The opiate throb and ache that was his wound.
Water – calm, sliding green above the weir.
Water – a sky-lit alley for his boat,
Bird-voiced, and bordered with reflected flowers
And shaken hues of summer: drifting down,
He dipped contented oars, and sighed, and slept.

Night, with a gust of wind, was in the ward,
Blowing the curtain to a glimmering curve.
Night. He was blind; he could not see the stars
Glinting among the wraiths of wandering cloud;
Queer blots of colour, purple, scarlet, green,
Flickered and faded in his drowning eyes.

Rain – he could hear it rustling through the dark;
Fragrance and passionless music woven as one;
Warm rain on drooping roses; pattering showers
That soak the woods; not the harsh rain that sweeps
Behind the thunder, but a trickling peace,
Gently and slowly washing life away.

He stirred, shifting his body; then the pain
Leapt like a prowling beast, and gripped and tore
His groping dreams with grinding claws and fangs.
But someone was beside him; soon he lay
Shuddering because that evil thing had passed.
And death, who'd stepped toward him,

                                paused and stared.

Light many lamps and gather round his bed.
Lend him your eyes, warm blood, and will to live.
Speak to him; rouse him; you may save him yet.
He's young; he hated War; how should he die
When cruel old campaigners win safe through?

But death replied: 'I choose him.' So he went,
And there was silence in the summer night;
Silence and safety; and the veils of sleep.
Then, far away, the thudding of the guns.

William Orpen, 'The Gunners' Shelter, Thiepval'

HERO

'JACK fell as he'd have wished,' the Mother said,
And folded up the letter that she'd read.
'The Colonel writes so nicely.' Something broke
In the tired voice that quavered to a choke.
She half looked up. 'We mothers are so proud
Of our dead soldiers.' Then her face was bowed.

Quietly the Brother Officer went out.
He'd told the poor old dear some gallant lies
That she would nourish all her days, no doubt.
For while he coughed and mumbled, her weak eyes
Had shone with gentle triumph, brimmed with joy,
Because he'd been so brave, her glorious boy.

He thought how 'Jack', cold-footed, useless swine,
Had panicked down the trench that night the mine
Went up at Wicked Corner; how he'd tried
To get sent home, and how, at last, he died,
Blown to small bits. And no one seemed to care
Except that lonely woman with white hair.

ATTACK

A T dawn the ridge emerges massed and dun
In the wild purple of the glowering sun,
Smouldering through spouts of drifting smoke

that shroud

The menacing scarred slope; and, one by one,
Tanks creep and topple forward to the wire.
The barrage roars and lifts. Then, clumsily bowed
With bombs and guns and shovels and battle-gear,
Men jostle and climb to meet the bristling fire.
Lines of grey, muttering faces, masked with fear,
They leave their trenches, going over the top,
While time ticks blank and busy on their wrists,
And hope, with furtive eyes and grappling fists,
Flounders in mud. O Jesus, make it stop!

THE REDEEMER

D ARKNESS: the rain sluiced down; the mire was deep;
It was past twelve on a mid-winter night,
When peaceful folk in beds lay snug asleep;
There, with much work to do before the light,
We lugged our clay-sucked boots as best we might
Along the trench; sometimes a bullet sang,
And droning shells burst with a hollow bang;
We were soaked, chilled and wretched, every one;
Darkness; the distant wink of a huge gun.

I turned in the black ditch, loathing the storm;
A rocket fizzed and burned with blanching flare,
And lit the face of what had been a form
Floundering in mirk. He stood before me there;
I say that He was Christ; stiff in the glare;
And leaning forward from His burdening task,
Both arms supporting it; His eyes on mine
Stared from the woeful head that seemed a mask
Of mortal pain in Hell's unholy shine.

No thorny crown, only a woollen cap
He wore – an English soldier, white and strong,
Who loved his time like any simple chap,
Good days of work and sport and homely song;
Now he has learned that nights are very long,
And dawn a watching of the windowed sky.
But to the end, unjudging, he'll endure
Horror and pain, not uncontent to die
That Lancaster on Lune may stand secure.

He faced me, reeling in his weariness,
Shouldering his load of planks, so hard to bear.
I say that He was Christ, who wrought to bless
All groping things with freedom bright as air,
And with His mercy washed and made them fair.
Then the flame sank, and all grew black as pitch,
While we began to struggle along the ditch;
And someone flung his burden in the muck,
Mumbling: 'O Christ Almighty, now I'm stuck!'

PRELUDE: THE TROOPS

Dim, gradual thinning of the shapeless gloom
Shudders to drizzling daybreak that reveals
Disconsolate men who stamp their sodden boots
And turn dulled, sunken faces to the sky
Haggard and hopeless. They, who have beaten down
The stale despair of night, must now renew
Their desolation in the truce of dawn,
Murdering the livid hours that grope for peace.

Yet these who cling to life with stubborn hands,
Can grin through storms of death and find a gap
In the clawed, cruel tangles of his defence.
They march from safety, and the bird-sung joy
Of grass-green thickets, to the land where all
Is ruin, and nothing blossoms but the sky
That hastens over them where they endure
Sad, smoking, flat horizons, recking woods,
And foundered trench-lines volleying doom for doom.

O my brave brown companions, when your souls
Flock silently away, and the eyeless dead
Shame the wild beast of battle on the ridge,
Death will stand grieving in that field of war
Since your unvanquished hardihood is spent.
And through some mooned Valhalla there will pass
Battalions and battalions, scarred from hell;
The unreturning army that was youth;
The legions who have suffered and are dust.

SURVIVORS

No doubt they'll soon get well; the shock and strain
Have caused their stammering, disconnected talk.
Of course they're 'longing to go out again' —
These boys with old, scared faces, learning to walk.
They'll soon forget their haunted nights; their cowed
Subjection to the ghosts of friends who died —
Their dreams that drip with murder; and they'll be proud
Of glorious war that shatter'd all their pride ...
Men who went out to battle, grim and glad;
Children, with eyes that hate you, broken and mad.

FIGHT TO A FINISH

The boys came back.
          Bands played and flags were flying,
And Yellow-Pressmen thronged the sunlit street
To cheer the soldiers who'd refrained from dying,
And hear the music of returning feet.
'Of all the thrills and ardours War has brought,
This moment is the finest.' (So they thought.)

Snapping their bayonets on to charge the mob,
Grim Fusiliers broke ranks with glint of steel,
At last the boys had found a cushy job.

I heard the Yellow-Pressmen grunt and squeal;
And with my trusty bombers turned and went
To clear those Junkers out of Parliament.

MEMORIAL TABLET

SQUIRE nagged and bullied till I went to fight
(Under Lord Derby's scheme). I died in hell –
(They called it Passchendaele). My wound was slight,
And I was hobbling back; and then a shell
Burst slick upon the duck-boards: so I fell
Into the bottomless mud, and lost the light.

At sermon-time, while Squire is in his pew,
He gives my gilded name a thoughtful stare;
For, though low down upon the list, I'm there:
'*In proud and glorious memory*' ... that's my due.
Two bleeding years I fought in France for Squire;
I suffered anguish that he's never guessed.
Once I came home on leave; and then went west.
What greater glory could a man desire?

DOES IT MATTER?

DOES it matter? – losing your legs?
For people will always be kind,
And you need not show that you mind
When others come in after hunting
To gobble their muffins and eggs.

Does it matter? – losing your sight?
There's such splendid work for the blind;
And people will always be kind,
As you sit on the terrace remembering
And turning your face to the light.

Do they matter? – those dreams in the pit?
You can drink and forget and be glad,
And people won't say that you're mad;
For they know that you've fought for your country,
And no one will worry a bit.

COUNTER-ATTACK

WE'D gained our first objective hours before
While dawn broke like a face with blinking eyes,
Pallid, unshaved and thirsty, blind with smoke.
Things seemed all right at first. We held their line,
With bombers posted, Lewis guns well placed,
And clink of shovels deepening the shallow trench.
The place was rotten with dead; green clumsy legs
High-booted, sprawled and grovelled along the saps
And trunks, face downward, in the sucking mud,
Wallowed like trodden sand-bags loosely filled;
And naked sodden buttocks, mats of hair,
Bulged, clotted heads slept in the plastering slime.
And then the rain began – the jolly old rain!

A yawning soldier knelt against the bank,
Staring across the morning blear with fog;
He wondered when the Allemands would get busy;
And then, of course, they started with five-nines
Traversing, sure as fate, and never a dud.
Mute in the clamour of shells he watched them burst
Spouting dark earth and wire with gusts from hell,
While posturing giants dissolved in drifts of smoke.
He crouched and flinched, dizzy with galloping fear,
Sick for escape – loathing the strangled horror
And butchered, frantic gestures of the dead.

An officer came blundering down the trench:
'Stand-to and man the fire-step!' On he went...
Gasping and bawling, 'Fire-step ... counter-attack!'
Then the haze lifted. Bombing on the right
Down the old sap: machine-guns on the left;
And stumbling figures looming out in front.
'O Christ, they're coming at us!' Bullets spat,
And he remembered his rifle ... rapid fire ...
And started blazing wildly ... then a bang
Crumpled and spun him sideways, knocked him out
To grunt and wriggle: none heeded him; he choked
And fought the flapping veils of smothering gloom,
Lost in a blurred confusion of yells and groans ...
Down, and down, and down, he sank and drowned,
Bleeding to death. The counter-attack had failed.

EVERYONE SANG

EVERYONE suddenly burst out singing;
And I was filled with such delight
As prisoned birds must find in freedom,
Winging wildly across the white
Orchards and dark-green fields;
                              on – on – and out of sight.

Everyone's voice was suddenly lifted;
And beauty came like the setting sun:
My heart was shaken with tears; and horror
Drifted away ... O, but Everyone
Was a bird; and the song was wordless;
                              the singing will never be done.

THE REAR-GUARD

GROPING along the tunnel, step by step,
He winked his prying torch with patching glare
From side to side, and sniffed the unwholesome air.

Tins, boxes, bottles, shapes too vague to know,
A mirror smashed, the mattress from a bed;
And he, exploring fifty feet below
The rosy gloom of battle overhead.
Tripping, he gripped the wall; saw someone lie
Humped at his feet, half-hidden by a rug,
And stooped to give the sleeper's arm a tug.
'I'm looking for headquarters.' No reply.
'God blast your neck!' (For days he'd had no sleep.)
'Get up and guide me through this stinking place.'
Savage, he kicked a soft, unanswering heap,
And flashed his beam across the livid face
Terribly glaring up, whose eyes yet wore
Agony dying hard ten days before;
And fists of fingers clutched a blackening wound.

Alone he staggered on until he found
Dawn's ghost that filtered down a shafted stair
To the dazed, muttering creatures underground
Who hear the boom of shells in muffled sound.
At last, with sweat of horror in his hair,
He climbed through darkness to the twilight air,
Unloading hell behind him step by step.

A WORKING PARTY

THREE hours ago he blundered up the trench,
  Sliding and poising, groping with his boots;
Sometimes he tripped and lurched against the walls
With hands that pawed the sodden bags of chalk.
He couldn't see the man who walked in front;
Only he heard the drum and rattle of feet
Stepping along barred trench boards, often splashing
Wretchedly where the sludge was ankle-deep.

Voices would grunt 'Keep to your right – make way!'
When squeezing past some men from the front-line:
White faces peered, puffing a point of red;
Candles and braziers glinted through the chinks
And curtain-flaps of dug-outs; then the gloom
Swallowed his sense of sight; he stooped and swore
Because a sagging wire had caught his neck.

A flare went up; the shining whiteness spread
And flickered upward, showing nimble rats
And mounds of glimmering sand-bags,
                                    bleached with rain;
Then the slow silver moment died in dark.
The wind came posting by with chilly gusts
And buffeting at the corners, piping thin.
And dreary through the crannies; rifle-shots
Would split and crack and sing along the night,
And shells came calmly through the drizzling air
To burst with hollow bang below the hill.

Three hours ago he stumbled up the trench;
Now he will never walk that road again:
He must be carried back, a jolting lump
Beyond all needs of tenderness and care.

He was a young man with a meagre wife
And two small children in a Midland town;
He showed their photographs to all his mates,
And they considered him a decent chap
Who did his work and hadn't much to say,
And always laughed at other people's jokes
Because he hadn't any of his own.

That night when he was busy at his job
Of piling bags along the parapet,
He thought how slow time went, stamping his feet
And blowing on his fingers, pinched with cold.
He thought of getting back by half-past twelve,
And tot of rum to send him warm to sleep
In draughty dug-out frowsty with the fumes
Of coke, and full of snoring weary men.

He pushed another bag along the top,
Craning his body outward; then a flare
Gave one white glimpse of No Man's Land and wire;
And as he dropped his head the instant split
His startled life with lead, and all went out.

GLORY OF WOMEN

You love us when we're heroes, home on leave,
Or wounded in a mentionable place.
You worship decorations; you believe
That chivalry redeems the war's disgrace.
You make us shells. You listen with delight,
By tales of dirt and danger fondly thrilled.
You crown our distant ardours while we fight,
And mourn our laurelled memories when we're killed.
You can't believe that British troops 'retire'
When hell's last horror breaks them, and they run,
Trampling the terrible corpses – blind with blood.
O German mother dreaming by the fire,
While you are knitting socks to send your son
His face is trodden deeper in the mud.

SUICIDE IN THE TRENCHES

I KNEW a simple soldier boy
Who grinned at life in empty joy,
Slept soundly through the lonesome dark,
And whistled early with the lark.

In winter trenches, cowed and glum,
With crumps and lice and lack of rum,
He put a bullet through his brain.
No one spoke of him again.

You smug-faced crowds with kindling eye
Who cheer when soldier lads march by,
Sneak home and pray you'll never know
The hell where youth and laughter go.

Alan Seeger (1888–1916)

RENDEZVOUS

I HAVE a rendezvous with Death
At some disputed barricade,
When Spring comes back with rustling shade
And apple-blossoms fill the air –
I have a rendezvous with Death
When Spring brings back blue days and fair.

It may be he shall take my hand
And lead me into his dark land
And close my eyes and quench my breath –
It may be I shall pass him still.
I have a rendezvous with Death
On some scarred slope of battered hill,
When Spring comes round again this year
And the first meadow-flowers appear.

God knows 'twere better to be deep
Pillowed in silk and scented down,
Where Love throbs out in blissful sleep,
Pulse nigh to pulse, and breath to breath,
Where hushed awakenings are dear ...
But I've a rendezvous with Death
At midnight in some flaming town,
When Spring trips north again this year,
And I to my pledged word am true.
I shall not fail that rendezvous.

Charles Hamilton Sorley (1895–1915)

WHEN YOU SEE MILLIONS OF THE MOUTHLESS DEAD

WHEN you see millions of the mouthless dead
  Across your dreams in pale battalions go,
Say not soft things as other men have said,
That you'll remember. For you need not so.
Give them not praise. For, deaf, how should they know
It is not curses heaped on each gashed head?
Nor tears. Their blind eyes see not your tears flow.
Nor honour. It is easy to be dead.
Say only this, 'They are dead.' Then add thereto,

'Yet many a better one has died before.'
Then, scanning all the overcrowded mass, should you
Perceive one face that you loved heretofore,
It is a spook. None wears the face you knew.
Great death has made all this for evermore.

Two Sonnets (I)

SAINTS have adored the lofty soul of you.
Poets have whitened at your high renown.
We stand among the many millions who
Do hourly wait to pass your pathway down.
You, so familiar, once were strange: we tried
To live as of your presence unaware.
But now in every road on every side
We see your straight and steadfast signpost there.

I think it like that signpost in my land,
Hoary and tall, which pointed me to go
Upward, into the hills, on the right hand,
Where the mists swim and the winds shriek and blow,
A homeless land and friendless, but a land
I did not know and that I wished to know.

TWO SONNETS (II)

SUCH, such is Death: no triumph: no defeat:
Only an empty pail, a slate rubbed clean,
A merciful putting away of what has been.

And this we know: Death is not Life effete,
Life crushed, the broken pail. We who have seen
So marvellous things know well the end not yet.

Victor and vanquished are a-one in death:
Coward and brave: friend, foe. Ghosts do not say,
'Come, what was your record when you drew breath?'
But a big blot has hid each yesterday
So poor, so manifestly incomplete.
And your bright Promise, withered long and sped,
Is touched, stirs, rises, opens and grows sweet
And blossoms and is you, when you are dead.

Edward Thomas (1878–1917)

THE CHERRY TREES

THE cherry trees bend over and are shedding,
  On the old road where all that passed are dead,
Their petals, strewing the grass as for a wedding
This early May morn when there is none to wed.

AS THE TEAM'S HEAD-BRASS

As the team's head-brass flashed out on the turn
  The lovers disappeared into the wood.
I sat among the boughs of the fallen elm
That strewed the angle of the fallow, and
Watched the plough narrowing a yellow square
Of charlock. Every time the horses turned
Instead of treading me down, the ploughman leaned
Upon the handles to say or ask a word,
About the weather, next about the war.
Scraping the share he faced towards the wood,
And screwed along the furrow till the brass flashed
Once more.

The blizzard felled the elm whose crest
I sat in, by a woodpecker's round hole,
The ploughman said. 'When will they take it away?'
'When the war's over.' So the talk began –
One minute and an interval of ten,
A minute more and the same interval.
'Have you been out?' 'No.'
                              'And don't want to, perhaps?'
'If I could only come back again, I should.
I could spare an arm. I shouldn't want to lose
A leg. If I should lose my head, why, so,
I should want nothing more ... Have many gone
From here?' 'Yes.' 'Many lost?' 'Yes, a good few.
Only two teams work on the farm this year.
One of my mates is dead. The second day
In France they killed him. It was back in March,
The very night of the blizzard, too. Now if
He had stayed here we should have moved the tree.'
'And I should not have sat here. Everything
Would have been different. For it would have been
Another world.' 'Ay, and a better, though
If we could see all all might seem good.' Then
The lovers came out of the wood again:
The horses started and for the last time
I watched the clods crumble and topple over
After the ploughshare and the stumbling team.

GONE, GONE AGAIN

Gone, gone again,
May, June, July,
And August gone,
Again gone by,

Not memorable
Save that I saw them go,
As past the empty quays
The rivers flow.

And now again,
In the harvest rain,
The Blenheim oranges
Fall grubby from the trees

As when I was young –
And when the lost one was here –
And when the war began
To turn young men to dung.

Look at the old house,
Outmoded, dignified,
Dark and untenanted,
With grass growing instead

Of the footsteps of life,
The friendliness, the strife;
In its beds have lain
Youth, love, age, and pain:

I am something like that;
Only I am not dead,
Still breathing and interested
In the house that is not dark:

I am something like that:
Not one pane to reflect the sun,
For the schoolboys to throw at —
They have broken every one.

RAIN

RAIN, midnight rain, nothing but the wild rain
On this bleak hut, and solitude, and me
Remembering again that I shall die
And neither hear the rain nor give it thanks
For washing me cleaner than I have been
Since I was born into this solitude.
Blessed are the dead that the rain rains upon:
But here I pray that none whom once I loved
Is dying tonight or lying still awake
Solitary, listening to the rain,
Either in pain or thus in sympathy
Helpless among the living and the dead,
Like a cold water among broken reeds,
Myriads of broken reeds all still and stiff,
Like me who have no love which this wild rain
Has not dissolved except the love of death,
If love it be for what is perfect and
Cannot, the tempest tells me, disappoint.

This Is No Case of Petty Right or Wrong

THIS is no case of petty right or wrong
   That politicians or philosophers
Can judge. I hate not Germans, nor grow hot
With love of Englishmen, to please newspapers.
Beside my hate for one fat patriot
My hatred of the Kaiser is love true:
A kind of god he is, banging a gong.
But I have not to choose between the two,
Or between justice and injustice. Dinned
With war and argument I read no more
Than in the storm smoking along the wind
Athwart the wood. Two witches' caldrons roar.
From one the weather shall rise clear and gay;
Out of the other an England beautiful
And like her mother that died yesterday.
Little I know or care if, being dull,
I shall miss something that historians
Can rake out of the ashes with perchance
The phoenix broods serene above their ken.
But with the best and meanest Englishmen
I am one in crying, God save England, lest
We lose what never slaves and cattle blessed.
The ages made her that made us from dust:
She is all we know and live by, and we trust
She is good and must endure, loving her so:
And as we love ourselves we hate her foe.

A PRIVATE

THIS ploughman dead in battle slept out of doors
   Many a frozen night, and merrily
Answered staid drinkers, good bedmen, and all bores:
'At Mrs Greenland's Hawthorn Bush,' said he,
'I slept.' None knew which bush. Above the town,
Beyond 'The Drover', a hundred spot the down
In Wiltshire. And where now at last he sleeps
More sound in France – that, too, he secret keeps.

THE OWL

DOWNHILL I came, hungry, and yet not starved;
   Cold, yet had heat within me that was proof
Against the North wind; tired, yet so that rest
Had seemed the sweetest thing under a roof.

Then at the inn I had food, fire, and rest,
Knowing how hungry, cold, and tired was I.
All of the night was quite barred out except
An owl's cry, a most melancholy cry

Shaken out long and clear upon the hill,
No merry note, nor cause of merriment,
But one telling me plain what I escaped
And others could not, that night, as in I went.

And salted was my food, and my repose,
Salted and sobered, too, by the bird's voice
Speaking for all who lay under the stars,
Soldiers and poor, unable to rejoice.

LIGHTS OUT

I HAVE come to the borders of sleep,
The unfathomable deep
Forest, where all must lose
Their way, however straight,
Or winding, soon or late;
They cannot choose.

Many a road and track
That, since the dawn's first crack,
Up to the forest brink,
Deceived the travellers,
Suddenly now blurs,
And in they sink.

Here love ends —
Despair, ambition ends;
All pleasure and all trouble,
Although most sweet or bitter,
Here ends in sleep that is sweeter
Than tasks most noble.

There is not any book
Or face of dearest look
That I would not turn from now
To go into the unknown
I must enter and leave alone,
I know not how.

The tall forest towers;
Its cloudy foliage lowers
Ahead, shelf above shelf;
Its silence I hear and obey
That I may lose my way
And myself.

IN MEMORIAM (EASTER, 1915)

THE flowers left thick at nightfall in the wood
This Eastertide call into mind the men,
Now far from home, who, with their sweethearts, should
Have gathered them and will do never again.

Sir William Watson (1858–1935)

TO THE TROUBLER OF THE WORLD

At last we know you, War-lord. You that flung
The gauntlet down, fling down the mask you wore,
Publish your heart, and let its pent hate pour,
You that had God for ever on your tongue.
We are old in war, and if in guile we are young,
Young also is the spirit that evermore
Burns in our bosom ev'n as heretofore,
Nor are these thews unbraced, these nerves unstrung.
We do not with God's name make wanton play;
We are not on such easy terms with Heaven;
But in Earth's hearing we can verily say,
'Our hands are pure; for peace,
                                            for peace we have striven.'
And not by Earth shall he be soon forgiven
Who lit the fire accurst that flames today.

T.P. Cameron Wilson (1889–1918)

STILL

Still though chaos
Works on the ancient plan;
Two things have changed not
Since first the world began.
The beauty of the wild green earth
And the bravery of man.

W.B. Yeats (1865–1939)

AN IRISH AIRMAN FORESEES HIS DEATH

I KNOW that I shall meet my fate
Somewhere among the clouds above;
Those that I fight I do not hate,
Those that I guard I do not love;
My country is Kiltartan Cross,
My countrymen Kiltartan's poor,
No likely end could bring them loss
Or leave them happier than before.
Nor law, nor duty bade me fight,
Nor public men, nor cheering crowds,
A lonely impulse of delight
Drove to this tumult in the clouds;
I balanced all, brought all to mind,
The years to come seemed waste of breath,
A waste of breath the years behind
In balance with this life, this death.

ON BEING ASKED FOR A WAR POEM

I THINK it better that in times like these
A poet's mouth should be silent, for in truth
We have no gift to set a statesman right;
He has had enough of meddling who can please
A young girl in the indolence of her youth,
Or an old man upon a winter's night.

Index of First Lines

John Singer Sargent, 'Thou Shalt Not Steal'

Acknowledgements

For permission to reprint copyright material, the publishers gratefully acknowledge the following:

Rosica Colin for Richard Aldington's 'The Lover' and 'Bombardment', copyright © Estate of Richard Aldington;

PFD (www.pfd.co.uk) on behalf of the Estate of Mrs Claire Blunden for Edmund Blunden's 'The Midnight Skaters' (from *English Poems*, copyright © Estate of Mrs Claire Blunden 1925), 'Vlamertinghe: Passing the Chateau' and 'Preparations for Victory' (from *Undertones of War*, copyright © Estate of Mrs Claire Blunden 1928), and 'Report on Experience' (from *Near and Far*, copyright © Estate of Mrs Claire Blunden 1929);

Major James C. Slater for May Wedderburn Cannan's 'Lamplight';

Pan Macmillan for Wilfrid Gibson's 'Mad', 'Breakfast', and 'Mark Anderson';

Carcanet Press Ltd for Ivor Gurney's 'To His Love', 'The Bohemians', 'The Target', 'The Silent One', 'Strange Hells', 'Tobacco', and 'Song';

A.P. Watt Ltd on behalf of the National Trust for Places of Historical Interest and Natural Beauty for Rudyard Kipling's 'For All We Have and Are', 'My Boy Jack', 'Gethsemane', 'Common Form', and 'A Dead Statesman';

The Barbara Levy Literary Agency and Mr George Sassoon for Siegfried Sassoon's 'They', 'A Subaltern', 'Dreamers', 'The Death-Bed', 'Attack', 'The Redeemer', 'Hero', 'Prelude: The Troops', 'Survivors', 'Fight to a Finish', 'Memorial Tablet', 'Does It Matter?', 'Counter-Attack', 'Everyone Sang', 'A Working Party', 'The Rear-Guard', 'Glory of Women', and 'Suicide in the Trenches';

A.P. Watt Ltd on behalf of Michael B. Yeats for W.B. Yeats's 'An Irish Airman Foresees His Death' and 'On Being Asked for a War Poem'.

In this anthology, the publishers have made every effort to trace the copyright holders of all illustrations and poems in copyright. They would be interested to hear from any copyright holders not here acknowledged.